John Frost, George Washington

Lives Of The Heroes Of The American Revolution

Comprising The Lives Of Washington And His Generals

John Frost, George Washington

Lives Of The Heroes Of The American Revolution
Comprising The Lives Of Washington And His Generals

ISBN/EAN: 9783337115746

Printed in Europe, USA, Canada, Australia, Japan

Cover: Foto ©ninafisch / pixelio.de

More available books at **www.hansebooks.com**

LIVES OF THE HEROES

OF THE

AMERICAN REVOLUTION:

COMPRISING

THE LIVES OF WASHINGTON AND HIS GENERALS
AND OFFICERS WHO WERE THE MOST DIS
TINGUISHED IN THE WAR OF THE IN-
DEPENDENCE OF THE U. S. A.;

ALSO—EMBRACING

THE DECLARATION OF INDEPENDENCE

AND SIGNERS' NAMES;

THE CONSTITUTION OF THE UNITED STATES

AND AMENDMENTS;

TOGETHER WITH THE INAUGURAL, FIRST ANNUAL
AND FAREWELL ADDRESSES OF WASHINGTON.

Embellished with Portraits.

PHILADELPHIA:
G. G. EVANS, PUBLISHER,
No. 439 CHESTNUT STREET,
1860.

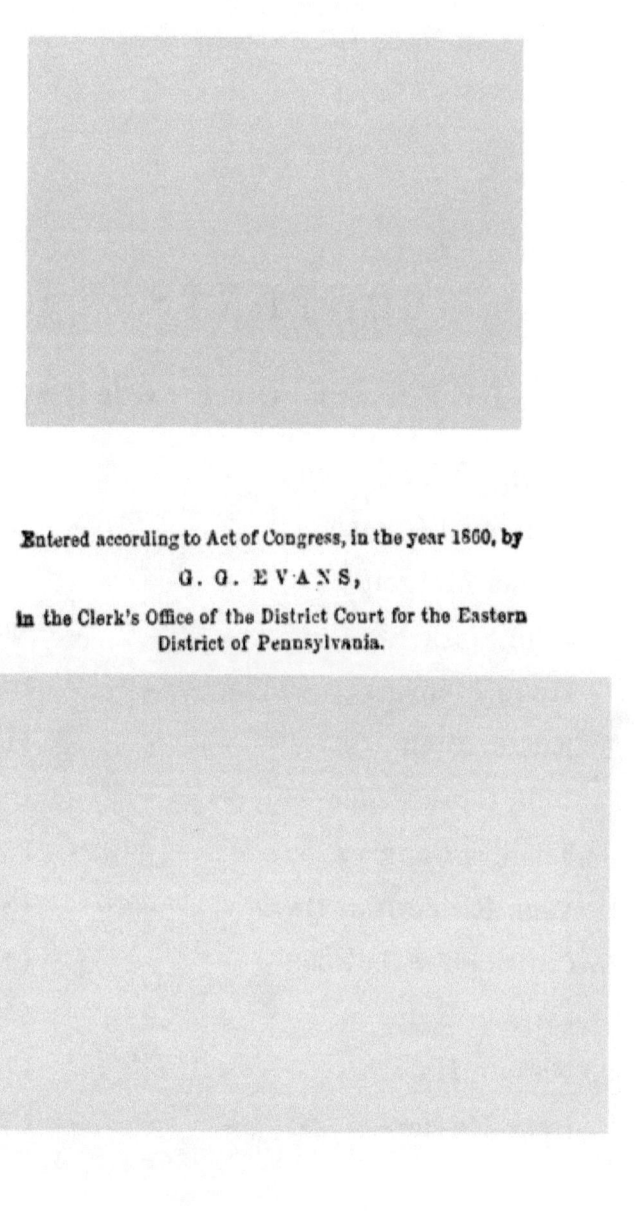

Entered according to Act of Congress, in the year 1860, by

G. G. EVANS,

in the Clerk's Office of the District Court for the Eastern District of Pennsylvania.

CONTENTS.

LIVES OF OFFICERS.

	Page
George Washington	7
Nathaniel Greene	27
Daniel Morgan	76
John Stark	90
Hugh Mercer	106
Ethan Allen	115
John Cadwalader	126
Thomas Conway	130
Wm. Richardson Davie	134
Christopher Gadsden	142
Horatio Gates	151
Nathan Hale	173
Isaac Hayne	179

CONTENTS.

	Page
Charles Lee	184
John Sullivan	201
Joseph Warren	208
John Laurens	231
Thomas Mifflin	239
Gilbert Mottier Lafayette	241
Declaration of Independence	286
Constitution of the United States	295
Amendments to the Constitution	318
Washington's Inaugural Address	324
Washington's First Annual Address	332
Washington's Farewell Address	339

THE
HEROES OF THE REVOLUTION

GEORGE WASHINGTON.

GEORGE WASHINGTON was born on the 22d of February, 1732, on the banks of the river Potomac, in Virginia. His father dying when he was ten years old, he received a plain but useful education at the hands of his mother. He soon manifested a serious and contemplative disposition, and in his thirteenth year drew up a code of regulations for his own guidance, in which the germs are visible of those high principles which regulated his conduct in mature life. As a boy, he conceived a liking for the naval service, but, being dissuaded from this, he qualified himself for the occupation of a land-surveyor; and, at the age of eighteen, obtained, through his relation, Lord Fairfax, the office of Surveyor of the Western District of Virginia. This introduced him to the notice of Governor Dinwiddie, and in the following year he was appointed one of the Adjutant-Generals of Virginia, with the duty of training the militia.

The boundaries of the British and French possessions in America were at that time subjects of dispute. In 1753 Washington was sent on a mission to the French settlement on the Ohio, which he executed successfully; and on his return published a journal of his route, which attracted much notice. In the following year he was less fortunate, being taken prisoner with his party, while in command of an expedition against the French. Being allowed to return home, he withdrew from the service, and went to reside at Mount Vernon, an estate which descended to him on the death of an elder brother. In 1755 he accepted the rank of Aide-de-camp to General Braddock, and was present at the surprise of the British in the woods near the Monongahela, where his coolness, courage, and knowledge of Indian warfare, chiefly contributed to the preservation of a handful of the troops. He escaped unhurt, but had three horses killed under him, and his dress was four times pierced with rifle-balls. Having gained much credit by his conduct on this occasion, Washington was next employed to defend the western frontier against the incursions of the French and Indians. He concluded this harassing service at the end of four years, by reducing Fort du Quesne, and driving the French beyond the Ohio; and then resigned his commission.

After his return to Mount Vernon, in 1759, Washington married; and during the next fourteen years his time was divided between his duties as a member of the Colonial Assembly and agricultural pursuits, in which he took great interest. The disputes which preceded the Revolution again drew him from private life. He maintained that the Americans were entitled to all the rights of British subjects, and could not be taxed by a legislature in which they were not represented; and he recommended that, on the failure of peaceful and constitutional resistance, recourse should be had to arms. In 1774 the command of the troops raised by Virginia was given to him; and in 1775 he represented that State in the Convention held at Philadelphia. When the war began, Washington was chosen Commander-in-Chief of the American Army; an office which he accepted without remuneration, saying, that emolument would not have tempted him to forego the pleasures of private life, and that he should only require to have his expenses reimbursed. His private letters have since proved that his object, at that time, was not to procure separation from England; but his alacrity in entering into the contest, and his constancy throughout its continuance, refute the insinuation, only countenanced by certain forged letters, that he was not hearty in the cause of independence.

About fourteen thousand people were at this time collected around Boston, where General Gage was held in a state of siege. Washington reached the colonial camp in July, 1775, and proceeded to give to the assembled multitude the form and discipline of a regular force. His next endeavours were to extend the period for which men enlisting were obliged to serve, and to ensure the maintenance of the troops by appointing a Commissary-General to collect supplies, instead of depending for them on the voluntary and uncertain contributions of the several States. Neither of these wishes was complied with, and the want of every requisite obliged Washington to change the siege into a blockade, until the following March, when, having obtained artillery and engineers, he forced the English to give up the town and embark on board their fleet. His conduct during

this siege is admirable, both for the resolution
with which he maintained the blockade with
an inferior army composed of untried men, and
the patience with which he endured the re-
proaches of the people, to whom the real difficulties of his situation, with respect to arms
and ammunition, could not be disclosed. He
also established the principle, that captured
Americans should be treated as prisoners of war.

In April, 1776, Washington anticipated
the British in occupying New York, and the
adjacent islands. Before the arrival of
Lord Howe, in July, independence was pro-
claimed; and the American general refused to
negotiate unless acknowledged as the function-
ary of an independent government, saying, that
America, being her own mistress, and having
committed no fault, needed no pardon. A
severe defeat on Long Island, and subsequent
losses, compelled him to abandon the State of
New York to the English, to retreat with great
loss through New Jersey, and to take shelter
behind the Delaware, near Philadelphia. He
showed much skill in preventing the British
from taking advantage of these reverses, which
he sought to repair by surprising their posts at
Trenton and Princetown, in Jersey, where he

made many hundred prisoners. These successes were well timed, and revived the broken spirit of the country.

In 1777 Washington applied to Congress for more extensive powers, which were granted him, with the title of Dictator, by which he was empowered to act on his own responsibility in all military affairs. But he was not supplied with the means of acting effectually; and the campaign of that year was one of misfortunes, the Americans being defeated at Brandywine, and forced to yield Philadelphia to the English. During the winter months Washington occupied a fortified camp at Valley Forge, and his army, ill-supplied with ammunition and provisions, was daily in danger of being destroyed by hunger or the enemy. He freely expressed his opinion to Congress of their misconduct, and his remarks occasioned a faction which desired to displace him from his command, and to substitute General Gates; but this was never seriously attempted.

The campaign of 1778 was favourable to Washington; he recovered Philadelphia, and following Clinton in his retreat through New-Jersey, brought him to action at Monmouth. The issue of this engagement gave new confidence to the people, and completely restored him to the good will of Congress. During the years 1779 and 1780 the war was actively carried on in the South, and Carolina and Virginia were reduced by the British. In the autumn of 1780 Major Andre, who had been sent by Clinton to concert with Arnold measures for betraying the post at West Point, was seized within the American lines, and tried and hanged as a spy. Whatever were the merits or misfortunes of the British officer, the duty of Washington was too plain to be mistaken, and the obloquy he incurred in its performance was undeserved.

Washington had throughout contended that the country could only be delivered by raising a permanent army, and consolidating the union of the States, so as to form a vigorous government. Five years' experience had taught Congress the inefficiency of temporary armies, and they resolved to form a permanent one with a system of half-pay and pensions, as an inducement to enter the service. But as the government of each State was empowered to levy its own taxes, and conduct all the measures for carrying this resolve into effect, such delay was occasioned, that although Count

Rochambeau arrived from France in August, 1780, with an auxiliary force of five thousand men, the American army could not actively co-operate with him during that year.

The temporising policy pursued by the States had severely tried the constancy of Washington, but did not lead him to despair of final success. The army, suffering extreme want, was kept in the field chiefly by attachment to his person. Attentive to alleviate their hardships, he did not permit any disorderly license; and although early in 1781 he allowed Congress to pacify the revolted troops, he, on a second occasion, shortly after, forcibly compelled the mutineers to submit, and summarily tried and executed many of them.

The pecuniary aid of France, and increased activity of the American Government, enabled Washington to resume offensive measures in the summer of 1781. Earl Cornwallis, then in Virginia, and but feebly opposed by LaFayette, sent a part of his army to strengthen Clinton in New York. Shortly after De Grasse arrived off the coast of Virginia with a French fleet. Washington took advantage of this conjuncture to transfer the war to the South. Deceiving Clinton as to his real design, he marched rapidly through New Jersey and Maryland, and, embarking his army on the Chesapeake, effected a junction at Williamsburg with La Fayette. By the combined operation of their forces, assisted by the fleet under De Grasse, Lord Cornwallis was compelled to surrender at York Town, with his whole force, October 19, after a siege of thirteen days. This event decided the war; but Washington remained watchful to preserve the advantages gained, and to provide for future contingencies, until 1783, when a general peace was concluded.

Washington then prepared to resume his station as a private citizen. The army had become disaffected towards the States, and appeared not unwilling to subvert the freedom of their country, if the general had sought his own aggrandisement. But he nobly rejected all such schemes, and persuaded the soldiers to return home, and trust to the assurance of Congress for the discharge of the arrears due to them. Having publicly taken leave of his officers, he repaired to Annapolis, and December 23, 1783, appeared in Congress, and resigned his commission. He also presented the account of his receipts and expenditure during the late war, the items of which were entered in his own handwriting. His expenditure amounted to £19,306, and it subsequently appeared that he had applied considerable sums of his own to the public service, which he neglected to claim. He asked no favour or reward for himself, except that his letters should be free from postage, but he strongly recommended to Congress the claims of his late army.

Having delivered a farewell address to Congress, and forwarded one of a like character to the government of each State, pointing out the advantages they at present possessed, and giving his advice as to the future conduct of their affairs, he retired to Mount Vernon to enjoy the pleasures of private life. But although the next two years were passed in retirement, the mind of Washington was actively directed to public affairs. Beside maintaining a correspondence with the most eminent men, as well in Europe as in his own country, he was engaged in various projects to promote the agricultural and commercial interests of his native State. Under his direction, companies were formed to improve the navigation of the rivers James and Potomac, thus making Virginia the trading mart of the Western States. A number of shares in the James River Company, which were presented to him in 1785 by the legislature of Virginia, he employed in founding the college in Virginia, now called by his name. His deference to the popular feelings and prejudices on the subject of liberty was shown in his conduct with regard to the Cincinnati, a military society of which he was president, instituted to commemorate the occurrences of the late war. An outcry was raised that the honours conferred by this society being hereditary, a titled order would be created in the State. Washington therefore prevailed on the members to annul the offensive regulations, and to agree that the society should cease at the termination of their lives.

The want of union amongst the States, and the incapacity of the government, engaged the attention of every able man in America, and more especially interested Washington, who desired to witness the establishment of a great republic. The principal defect of the existing government was, that no acts of Congress in forming commercial treaties, borrowing money, or introducing national regulations, were binding on the individual States, each of which pursued its own interests, without showing any disposition to redeem the engagements of the government with the public creditors, either at home or abroad. Washington's principles were democratic; but he was opposed to those who contended for the absolute independence of the individual States, being convinced that each must sacrifice a portion of its liberty for the security of the whole, and that, without an energetic central government, the confederation would be insignificant. His representations to the Congress and the individual States, backed by the increasing distress of the country, at length brought about the Convention of Philadelphia, which met in May, 1787, and having chosen Washington president, continued sitting until September, when the federal constitution was finally decided on, and was submitted to the States for their approval.

Having acquitted himself of this duty, Washington retired to private life until March, 1789, when he was elected President of the United States. He had used no exertion to obtain this distinction, which his impaired health and love of retirement rendered unsuitable to him: he, however, accepted it, and his journey to New York was one continued triumph. April 30, he took the oaths prescribed by the constitution, and delivered his inaugural address, in which he dwelt most fully on his own reasons for again entering on public life, and on the duties incumbent upon members of the Congress. He declared that he would receive no remuneration for his services, and required that a stated sum should be allowed for defraying the expenses of his office.

The President of the Union being a new political personage, it became requisite to establish certain observances of etiquette towards him. Washington's arrangements in this respect were sufficiently simple, yet they excited jealousy, as savouring of regal and courtly customs. The restriction placed on the admission of idle visiters, who hourly intruded on him, caused much offence, and became the subject of remonstrance, even from intelligent men.

One of the first acts of Washington's administration was to empower the legislature to become responsible for the general debt of the States, and to levy taxes for the punctual discharge of the interest upon it. The operation of the new government was in every respect satisfactory, its beneficial influence being apparent in the increasing prosperity of the country; and before the end of the second year's presidency, Rhode Island and North Carolina, which at first were dissentient, desired to participate in the benefits of the Union, and were admitted as members. In 1790 Washington concluded a treaty with the hostile Indians on the Southern frontier; but the war which he directed against the Indians on the North Western frontier was unfortunate, the American forces sustaining three severe defeats Upon the whole, however, the period of his first presidency passed over prosperously and tranquilly. He was annoyed by occasional differences in his cabinet, and by the discontent of the anti-federal party; but being supported by John Adams, Hamilton, and other able men, his government suffered no real embarrassment.

In 1792, as he possessed the general confidence of the people, he was unanimously re-elected President; and in March, 1793, again took the oaths of office. The French Revolution was hailed with joy by the Americans, among whom an almost universal wish prevailed to assist in establishing, as they thought, true freedom in Europe. But Washington perceived that the real interests of his country required peace. He acknowledged the govern ment of the French Republic, and sent an ambassador to Paris; but declared his resolution to adopt a strict neutrality in the contest between France and the allied powers of Europe. Still the enthusiasm in favour of the French continued to increase; and, at the instigation of M. Genet, envoy from Paris, privateers were armed in the American ports, and sent to cruise against the British. Washington promptly suppressed this practice; and the conduct of Genet having been intemperate and insolent towards the President, and calculated to produce serious disturbance in the States, he took the requisite steps for having him recalled.

The determination of the President to preserve peace was not the only ground of popular discontent. The imposition of excise taxes, as they were termed by the people, excited serious murmurings; and, in 1794, a general rising took place in Pennsylvania, which was put down without bloodshed by a vigorous display of force, and the principals, after being condemned to death, were pardoned.

The ferment among the people made a war with England seemingly unavoidable. Washington, at this juncture, appointed Mr. Jay envoy to England, with full powers to conclude a treaty, in which all points then at issue between the two nations should be adjusted. With the concurrence of the Senate he ratified this treaty, regardless of the outcry raised against it; and subsequently upheld the authority of the President, in refusing to permit the House of Representatives to revise the articles it contained. The people soon perceived that the advantages to be derived from the contentions in Europe made it impolitic for their own country to become a party to them, and confidence and good will towards the President were in a great measure restored. These favourable dispositions were confirmed by the termination of a successful war against the Indians, and by a treaty with Spain, by which the navigation of the Mississippi to the Ocean was secured to the Americans.

Among the acts which immediately proceeded from Washington during his presidency, were those for forming a fund to pay off the national debt, and for organising the militia of the country. He was active and sssiduous in his duties as chief magistrate, making tours through the States, and ascertaining the progressive improvement in each, and the means which would most tend to increase it. The limited powers conferred on the President prevented his effecting so much as he desired, and the public measures originating from him were but few. He declined being nominated a third time to the office of President, and on his retirement published an address to the people of the United States, in which, after remarking on the condition and prospects of the country, he insisted on the necessity of cementing the union of the States, and upholding the supremacy of the Federal Government; he also advised them never to admit the influence of foreign powers, and to reap benefit from the quarrels amongst the States of Europe, by remaining at peace with all.

Washington passed the rest of his days at Mount Vernon, engaged in the society of his friends, and in the improvement of his estate. He was for several years a member of the British Agricultural Association; and the efforts he made to form a similar society in America, and his letters to Sir John Sinclair, (a fac-simile copy of which is deposited in the British Museum,) show the interest he took in agricultural affairs. He died December 13, 1799, in his sixty-eighth year, after a few days' illness, and was buried at Mount Vernon. He left no family. Congress suspended its sitting on receiving the intelligence of his death, and a public mourning was ordered for him.

In person, Washington was robust, and above the middle height. He was thoughtful and reserved, without being repulsive; and his manners were those of the old school of English gentlemen. Although mild and humane, he was stern in the performance of duty, and never, upon such occasions, yielded to softness or compassion. His speeches and official letters are simple and earnest, but wanting perhaps in that conciseness, which marks vigour of thought. Whilst President, he was assailed by the violence of party spirit. On his decease his worth was justly appreciated, and the sorrow at his loss was universal and sincere. Washington was distinguished less by the brilliancy of his talents than by his moral goodness, sound judgment, and plain but excellent understanding. His admirable use of those sterling, though homely qualities has gained a rank for him among the greatest and best of men; and his name will be coexistent, as it was coeval, with that of the empire, of which, no less by his rare civil wisdom than his eminent military talents, he may be considered the founder.

The virtues which distinguish him from all others who have united the fame of statesman and captain, were two-fold, and they are as great as they are rare. He refused power which his own merit had placed within his reach, constantly persisting in the preference of a republican to a monarchial form of government, as the most congenial to liberty when it is not incompatible with the habits of the people and the circumstances of society; and he even declined to continue longer than his years seemed to permit at the head of that commonwealth which he had founded. This subjugation of all ambitious feelings to the paramount sense of duty is his first excellence; it is the sacrifice of his own aggrandisement to his country's freedom. The next is like unto it; his constant love of peace when placed at the head of affairs: this was the sacrifice of the worthless glory which ordinary men prize the most, to the tranquillity and happiness of mankind. Wherefore to all ages and in all climes, they who most love public virtue will hold in eternal remembrance the name of

George Washington; never pronouncing it but with gratitude and awe, as designating a mortal removed above the ordinary lot of human frailty.

The words of his last will in bequeathing his sword to his nephews—the sword which he had worn in the sacred war of liberty—ought to be graven in letters of gold over every palace in the world: "This sword they shall never draw but in defence of freedom, or of their country, or of their kindred; and when thus drawn, they shall prefer falling with it in their hands to the relinquishment thereof."

For farther information we refer to the works of Ramsay and Marshall; and to the Correspondence of Washington, published by Mr. Sparkes.

NATHANIEL GREENE,

MAJOR-GENERAL IN THE AMERICAN ARMY.

GENERAL GREENE, although descended from ancestors of elevated standing, was not indebted to the condition of his family for any part of the real lustre and reputation he possessed. He was literally the founder of his own fortune, and the author of his own fame. He was the second son of Nathaniel Greene, a member of the society of Friends, an anchor-smith.

He was born in the year 1741, in the town of Warwick, and county of Kent, in the province of Rhode Island. Being intended by his father for the business which he himself pursued, young Greene received at school nothing but the elements of a common English education. But to him, an education so limited was unsatisfactory. With such funds as he was able to raise, he purchased a small, but well-selected library, and spent his evenings, and all the time he could redeem from his father's business, in regular study.

At a period of life unusually early, Greene was elevated, by a very flattering suffrage, to a seat in the legislature of his native colony. This was the commencement of a public career, which, heightening as it advanced, and flourishing in the midst of difficulties, closed with a lustre that was peculiarly dazzling.

Thus introduced into the councils of his country, at a time when the rights of the subject, and the powers of the ruler, were beginning to be topics of liberal discussion, he felt it his duty to avow his sentiments on the momentous question. Nor did he pause or waver, as to the principles he should adopt, and the decision he should form. He was inflexibly opposed to tyranny and oppression in every shape, and manfully avowed it. But his character, although forming, was not completely developed until the commencement of the troubles which terminated in our independence. It was then that he aspired to a head in the public councils; and throwing from him, as unsuitable to the times, the peaceful habits in which he had been educated, sternly declared for a redress of grievances, or open resistance. This open departure from the sectarian principles in which he had been educated, was followed, of course, by his immediate dismission from the society of Friends.

The sword was earliest unsheathed in the colony of Massachusetts; and on the plains of Lexington and Concord, the blood of British soldiers and American subjects mingled first in hostile strife. Nor was Rhode Island, after that sanguinary affair, behind her sister colonies, in gallantry of spirit and promptitude of preparation.

Greene commenced his military pupilage in the capacity of a *private soldier*, in October, 1774, in a military association, commanded by James M. Varnum, afterward brigadier-general. But Rhode Island having, in the month of May, 1775, raised three regiments of militia, she placed them under the command of Greene, who, without loss of time, conducted them to head-quarters, in the village of Cambridge.

On the 2d of July, 1775, General Washington, invested by Congress with the command in chief of the armies of his country, arrived at Boston. Greene availed himself of an early opportunity, amid the public demonstration of joy, to welcome the commander-in-chief, in a personal address, in which, with much warmth of feeling and kindness of expression, he avowed his attachment to his person, and the high gratification he derived from the prospect of being associated with him in arms, and serving under him in defence of the violated rights of his country.

This was a happy prelude to a friendship between these two great and illustrious officers, which death alone had the power to dissolve. It is a fact of notoriety, that when time and acquaintance had made him thoroughly acquainted with the character and merits of General Greene, Washington entertained, and frequently expressed, an anxious wish, that in case of his death he might be appointed his successor to the supreme command.

During the investment of Boston by the American forces, a state of things which lasted for months, no opportunity presented itself to Greene to acquire distinction by personal exploit. But his love of action, and spirit of adventure, were strongly manifested; for he was one of the few officers of rank who concurred with General Washington in the propriety of attempting to carry the town by assault.

On the evacuation of Boston by the British, the American troops were permitted to repose from their toils, and to exchange, for a time, the hardships and privations of a field encampment for the enjoyment of plenty in comfortable barracks. During this period of relaxation, Greene continued with unabating industry his military studies, and as far as opportunity served, his attention to the practical duties of the field. This course, steadily pursued, under the immediate supervision of Washington, could scarcely fail to procure rank, and lead to eminence. Accordingly, August 26, 1776, he was promoted by Congress to the rank of major-general in the regular army.

A crisis, most glowing and portentous to the cause of freedom, had now arrived. In the retreat which now commenced through New-Jersey, General Washington was accompanied by General Greene, and received from him all the aid that, under circumstances so dark and unpromising, talents, devotion, and firmness could afford. Possessed alike of an ardent temperament, hearts that neither danger nor misfortune could appal, and an inspiring trust in the righteousness of their cause, it belonged to the character of these two great and illustrious commanders, never for a moment to despair of their country. Hope and confidence, even now, beamed from their countenances, and they encouraged their followers, and supported them under the pressure of defeat and misfortune.

Greene was one of the council of Washington who resolved on the enterprise of December 26, 1776, against the post of the enemy at Trenton. The issue is known, and is glorious in our history. About one thousand Hessians, in killed, wounded, and prisoners, with their arms, field-equipage, and artillery, were the trophies of that glorious morning, which opened on the friends of American freedom with the day-star of hope. He was again of the council of the commander-in-chief, in planning the daring attack, January 2, 1777, on the British garrison at Princeton, as well as his associate in achieving its execution. In both these brilliant actions, his gallantry, prudence, and skill being alike conspicuous, he received the applauses of his commander. He continued the associate and most confidential counsellor of Washington through the gloomy and ominous period that followed.

In the obstinate and bloody battle of Brandywine, General Greene, by his distinguished conduct, added greatly to his former renown. In the course of it, a detachment of American troops, commanded by General Sullivan, being unexpectedly attacked by the enemy, retreated in disorder, General Greene, at the head of Weedon's Virginia brigade, flew to their support. On approaching, he found the defeat of General Sullivan a perfect rout. Not a moment was to be lost. Throwing himself into the rear of his flying countrymen, and retreating slowly, he kept up, especially from his cannon, so destructive a fire, as greatly to retard the advance of the enemy. Aiming at length at a narrow defile, secured on the right and left by thick woods, he halted, sent forward his cannon, that they might be out of danger, in case of his being compelled to a hasty retreat, and formed his troops, determined to dispute the pass with his small arms. This he effected with complete success, notwithstanding the vast superiority of the assailants; until, after a conflict of more than an hour and a half, night came on, and brought it to a close. But for this quick-sighted interposition, Sullivan's detachment must have been nearly annihilated.

On this occasion only did the slightest misunderstanding ever occur between General Greene and the commander-in-chief. In his general orders after the battle, the latter neglected to bestow any special applause on

Weedon's brigade. Against this General Greene remonstrated in person.

General Washington replied, "You, sir, are considered my favourite officer. Weedon's brigade, like myself, are Virginians. Should I applaud them for their achievement under your command, I shall be charged with partiality: jealousy will be excited, and the service injured."

"Sir," exclaimed Greene, with considerable emotion, "I trust your excellency will do me the justice to believe that I am not selfish. In my own behalf I have nothing to ask. Act towards *me* as you please; I shall not complain. However richly I prize your excellency's good opinion and applause, a consciousness that I have endeavoured to do my duty constitutes, at present, my richest reward. But do not, sir, let me entreat you, on account of the jealousy that may arise in little minds, withhold justice from the brave fellows I had the honour to command."

Convinced that prudence forbade the special notice requested, the commander-in-chief persisted in his silence. Greene, on cool reflection, appreciated the motive of his general, and lost no time in apologizing for his intemperate manner, if not for his expressions. Delighted with his frankness and magnanimity, Washington replied with a smile, "An officer, tried as you have been, who errs but once in two years, deserves to be forgiven." With that he offered him his hand, and the matter terminated.

Following General Greene in his military career, he next presents himself on the plains of Germantown. In this daring assault he commanded the left wing of the American army, and his utmost endeavours were used to retrieve the fortune of the day, in which his conduct met the approbation of the commander-in-chief. Lord Cornwallis, to whom he was often opposed, had the magnanimity to bestow upon him a lofty encomium. "Greene," said he, "is as dangerous as Washington. He is vigilant, enterprising, and full of resources. With but little hope of gaining any advantage over him, I never feel secure when encamped in his neighbourhood."

At this period the quartermaster department in the American army was in a very defective and alarming condition, and required a speedy and radical reform: and General Washington declared, that such reform could be effected only by the appointment of a quartermaster-general, of great resources, well versed in business, and possessing practical talents of the first order. When requested by Congress to look out for such an officer, he at once fixed his eye on General Greene.

Washington well knew that the soul of Greene was indissolubly wedded to the duties of his line. Notwithstanding this, he expressed, in conversation with a member of Congress, his entire persuasion, that if General Greene could be convinced of his ability to render his country greater services in the quartermaster department than in the field, he would at once accept the appointment. "There is not," said he, "an officer of the army, nor a man in America, more sincerely attached to the interests of his country. Could he best promote their interests in the character of a *corporal*, he would exchange, as I firmly believe, without a murmur, the epaulet for the knot. For although he is not without ambition, that ambition has not for its object the highest rank so much as the *greatest good*."

When the appointment was first offered to General Greene, he declined it; but after a conference with the commander-in-chief, he consented to an acceptance, on condition that he should forfeit nothing of his right to command in time of action. On these terms he received the appointment, March 22, 1778, and entered immediately on the duties of the office.

In this station he fully answered the expectations formed of his abilities; and enabled the American army to move with additional celerity and vigour.

During his administration of the quartermaster department, he took, on two occasions, a high and distinguished part in the field; the first in the battle of Monmouth; the second, in a very brilliant expedition against the enemy in Rhode Island, under the command of General Sullivan. At the battle of Monmouth, the commander-in-chief, disgusted with the behaviour of General Lee, deposed him in the field of battle, and appointed General Greene to command the right wing, where he greatly contributed to retrieve the errors of his predecessor, and to the subsequent events of the day.

His return to his native state was hailed by the inhabitants with general and lively demonstrations of joy. Even the leading members of the society of Friends, who had reluctantly excluded him from their communion, often visited him at his quarters, and expressed their sincere satisfaction at the elevation he had attained in the confidence of his country. One of these plain gentlemen being asked in jest, by a young officer, how he, as an advocate of peace, could reconcile it to his conscience to keep so much company with General Greene, whose profession was war? promptly replied, "Friend, it is not a suit of uniform that can either make or spoil a man. True, I do not approve of this many-coloured apparel, (to the officer's dress,) but whatever may be the form or colour of his coat, Nathaniel Greene still retains the same sound head and virtuous heart that gained him the love and esteem of our Society."

During the year 1779, General Greene was occupied exclusively in the extensive concerns of the quartermaster department.

About this time General Greene was called to the performance of a duty the most trying and painful he had ever encountered. We allude to the melancholy affair of Major Andre, adjutant-general to the British army, who was captured in disguise within the American lines. Washington detailed a court for this trial, composed of fourteen general officers, La

Fayette and Steuben being two of the number, and appointed General Greene to preside.

When summoned to his trial, Andre frankly disclosed, without interrogatory, what bore heaviest on his own life, but inviolably concealed whatever might endanger the safety of others. His confessions were conclusive, and no witness was examined against him. The court were unanimous that he had been taken as a spy, and must suffer death. Of this sentence he did not complain, but wished that he might be permitted to close a life of honour by a professional death, and not be compelled, like a common felon, to expire on a gibbet. To effect this, he made, in a letter to General Washington, one of the most powerful and pathetic appeals that ever fell from the pen of a mortal.

Staggered in his resolution, the commander-in-chief referred the subject, accompanied by the letter, to his general officers, who, with one exception, became unanimous in their desire that Andre should be shot.

That exception was found in General Greene, the president of the court. "Andre," said he, "is either a spy or an innocent man. If the latter, to execute him in any way will be murder: if the former, the mode of his death is prescribed by law, and you have no right to alter it. Nor is this all. At the present alarming crisis of our affairs, the public safety calls for a solemn and impressive example. Nothing can satisfy it short of the execution of the prisoner as a common spy; a character of which his own confession has clearly convicted him. Beware how you suffer your feelings to triumph over your judgment. Indulgence to one may be death to thousands. Besides, if you shoot the prisoner, instead of hanging him, you will excite suspicion which you will be unable to allay. Notwithstanding all your efforts to the contrary, you will awaken public compassion, and the belief will become general, that, in the case of Major Andre, there were exculpatory circumstances, entitling him to lenity, beyond what he received—perhaps entitling him to pardon. Hang him, therefore, or set him free."

This reasoning being considered conclusive, the prisoner suffered as a common spy.

We have now advanced to that period of the revolutionary war in which the situation of Greene is about to experience an entire change No longer acting in the vicinity, or subject to the immediate orders of a superior, we are to behold him, in future, removed to a distance, and virtually invested with the supreme command of a large section of the United States.

Congress, dissatisfied with the loss of the southern army, resolved that the conduct of General Gates be submitted to the examination of a court of inquiry, and the commander-in-chief directed to appoint an officer to succeed him. In compliance with the latter part of the resolution, General Washington, without hesitation, offered the appointment to General Greene. In a letter to Congress, recommending the general to the support of that body, he made the most honourable mention of him as "an officer in whose abilities, fortitude, and integrity, from a long and intimate experience of them, he had the most entire confidence." Writing to Mr. Matthews, a member from Charleston, he says, "You have your wish, in the officer appointed to the southern command. I think I am giving you a general; but what can a general do without arms, without clothing, without stores, without provisions?"

General Greene arrived at Charlotte, the head-quarters of General Gates, December 2, 1780, and in entering on the duties of his command, he found himself in a situation that was fearfully embarrassing. His army, consisting mostly of militia, amounted to less than two thousand men, and he found on hand but three days' provision, and a very defective supply of ammunition. In front was an enemy, proud in victory, and too strong to be encountered. With such means, and under such circumstances, to recover two states, already conquered, and protect a third, constituted a task that was almost hopeless.

It was not merely to meet an enemy in the field, to command skilfully and fight bravely, either in proffered or accepted battle. These operations depend on mere professional qualifications, that can be readily acquired by moderate capacities. But to raise and provide for an army in a dispirited and devastated country, creating resources where they do not exist; to operate with an incompetent force on an extended and broken line of frontier; to hold in check in many points, and to avoid coming into contact in any, with an enemy superior in numbers and discipline; to conduct a scheme of warfare like this—and such, precisely, was that which tested the abilities of General Greene—requires a genius of the highest order, combined with indefatigable industry and skill.

Preparatory to the commencement of the campaign, Greene's first care was to prepare for his troops subsistence and ammunition, and in effecting this, he derived great aid from his personal experience in the business of the commissary and quartermaster's departments. This qualification for such a diversity of duties, presented him to his troops in the two-fold relation of their supporter and commander. Much of the moral strength of an army consists in a confidence in its leader, an attachment to his person, and a spirit of subordination, founded on principle. To such an extent was this true, that even the common soldiery, sensible of the superintendence of a superior intellect, predicted confidently a change of fortune. Their defeat at Camden was soon forgotten by them in their anticipations of future victory. They fancied themselves ready once more to take the field, and felt a solicitude to regain their lost reputation, and signalize their prowess in presence of their new and beloved commander.

But, notwithstanding the spirit and confidence of his troops, Greene found himself unable to meet the enemy in the field. With Washington in his eye, and his own genius to devise his measures, he resolved on cautious movements and protracted war. Yet to sustain the spirit of the country, it was necessary that he should not altogether shun his enemy; but watching and confronting his scouts and foraging parties, fight, cripple, and beat him in detail; and in all his movements it was necessary for him to maintain a communication with Virginia, from which he was to receive supplies of provisions, munitions, and men.

General Greene's first movement from the village of Charlotte, was productive of the happiest effect. In the month of December he marched with his main army to the Cheraw Hills, about seventy miles to the right of Lord Cornwallis, despatching, at the same time, General Morgan, with four hundred continentals under Colonel Howard, Colonel Washington's corps of dragoons, and a few militia, amounting in all to six hundred, to take a position on the British left, distant from them about fifty miles.

This judicious disposition, which formed a rallying point for the friends of independence, both in the east and west, and facilitated the procurement of provisions for the troops, excited his lordship's apprehensions for the safety of Ninety-Six and Augusta, British posts, which he considered as menaced by the movements of Morgan, and gave rise to a train of movements which terminated in the celebrated battle of the Cowpens.

Cornwallis, immediately on learning the movements of Greene, despatched Colonel Tarlton with a strong detachment, amounting, in horse and foot, to near a thousand, for the protection of Ninety-Six, with orders to bring General Morgan, if possible, to battle. Greatly superior in numbers, he advanced on Morgan with a menacing aspect, and compelled him, at first, to fall back rapidly. But this was not long continued. Glorying in action, and relying with great confidence in the spirit and firmness of his regular troops, Morgan halted at the Cowpens, and prepared to give his adversary battle. The opportunity was eagerly seized by Tarlton. An engagement was the immediate consequence, and a complete victory was obtained by the Americans.* Upwards of five hundred of the British laid down their arms and were made prisoners, and a very con-

* Vide Biography of General Morgan.

siderable number were killed. Eight hundred stand of arms, two field-pieces, and thirty-five baggage wagons, fell to the victors, who had only twelve killed and sixty wounded.

The victory of the Cowpens, although achieved under the immediate command of Morgan, was the first stroke of General Greene's policy in the south, and augured favourably of his future career. It led to one of the most arduous, ably conducted, and memorable operations, that occurred in the course of the revolutionary war—the retreat of Greene, and the pursuit of Cornwallis, during the inclemencies of winter, a distance of two hundred and thirty miles.

Galled in his pride, and crippled in his schemes by the overthrow of Tarlton, Lord Cornwallis resolved, by a series of prompt and vigorous measures, to avenge the injury and retrieve the loss which the royal arms had sustained at the Cowpens. His meditated operations for this purpose were, to advance rapidly on Morgan, retake his prisoners, and destroy his force; to maintain an intermediate position, and prevent his union with General Greene or in case of the junction of the two armies, to cut off their retreat towards Virginia, and force them to action.

But General Greene, no less vigilant and provident than himself, informed, by express, of the defeat of Tarlton, instantly perceived the object of his lordship, and ordering his troops to proceed under General Huger to Salisbury, where he meditated a junction with Morgan's detachment, he himself, escorted by a few dragoons, set out for the head-quarters of that officer, and joined him shortly after.

Cornwallis having committed to the flames his heavy baggage, and reduced his army to the condition of light troops, dashed towards Morgan. And here commenced the retreat of General Greene, in the course of which he displayed such resources, and gained in the end such lasting renown. Sensible of the immense prize for which he was contending, he tasked his genius to the uttermost. On the issue of the struggle was staked, not merely the lives of a few brave men, not alone the existence of the whole army, but the fate of the south and the integrity of the Union. But his genius was equal to the crisis. By the most masterly movements, Greene effected a junction of the two divisions of his little army.

To his great mortification, Lord Cornwallis now perceived that in two of his objects, the destruction of Morgan's detachment, and the prevention of its union with the main division, he was completely frustrated by the activity of Greene. But to cut off the retreat of the Americans into Virginia, after their union, and to compel them to action, was still perhaps practicable, and to the achievement of this he now directed his undivided energies.

The genius of Greene, however, did not desert him on this trying occasion. Self-collected, and adapting his conduct to the nature of the crisis, his firmness grew with the increase of danger; and the measure of his greatness was the extent of the difficulties he was called to encounter. Notwithstanding the vigilance and activity of his enemy, he brought his men in safety into Virginia; and to crown the whole, no loss was sustained by him, either in men, munitions, artillery, or any thing that enters into the equipment of an army.

Frustrated thus in all his purposes, Lord Cornwallis, although the pursuing party, must be acknowledged to have been fairly vanquished. Victory is the successful issue of a struggle for superiority. Military leaders contend for different objects; to vanquish their enemies in open combat; to attack and overthrow them by stratagem and surprise; to exhaust their resources by delay of action; or to elude them in retreat, until, strengthened by reinforcements, they may be able to turn and meet them in the field. Of this last description was the victory of Greene in this memorable retreat.

In Virginia, General Greene received some reinforcements, and had the promise of more; on which he returned again into North Carolina, where, on their arrival, he hoped to be able to act on the offensive. He encamped in the vicinity of Lord Cornwallis's army. By a variety of the best concerted manœuvres, he so judiciously supported the arrangement of his troops, by the secrecy and promptitude of his motions, that during three weeks, while the enemy remained near him, he prevented them from taking any advantage of their superiority; and even cut off all opportunity of their receiving succours from the royalists.

About the beginning of March he effected a junction with a continental regiment and two considerable bodies of Virginia and Carolina militia. He then determined on attacking the

British commander without loss of time, " being persuaded," as he declared in his subsequent despatches, " that if he was successful, it would prove ruinous to the enemy ; and, if otherwise, that it would be but a partial evil to him." On the 14th he arrived at Guilford Court-House, the British then lying at twelve miles distance.

His army consisted of about four thousand five hundred men, of whom near two-thirds were North Carolina and Virginia militia. The British were about two thousand four hundred, all regular troops, and the greater part inured to toil and service in their long expedition under Lord Cornwallis, who, on the morning of the 15th, being apprised of General Greene's intentions, marched to meet him. The latter disposed his army in three lines : the militia of North Carolina were in front; the second line was composed of those of Virginia; and the third, which was the flower of the army, was formed of continental troops, near fifteen hundred in number. They were flanked on ooth sides by cavalry and riflemen, and posted on a rising ground, a mile and a half from Guilford Court-House.

"The engagement commenced at half an hour after one o'clock, by a brisk cannonade, after which the British advanced in three columns, and attacked the first line, composed of North Carolina militia. Those who probably had never been in action before, were panic-struck at the approach of the enemy; and many of them ran away without firing a gun, or being fired upon, and even before the British had come nearer than one hundred and forty yards to them. Part of them, however, fired; but they then followed the example of their comrades. Their officers made every possible effort to rally them; but neither the advantages of position, nor any other consideration, could induce them to maintain their ground. This shameful conduct had a great effect upon the issue of the battle. The next line, however, behaved much better. They fought with great bravery, and were thrown into disorder; rallied, returned to the charge, and kept up a heavy fire for a long time; but were at length broken and driven on the third line, when the engagement became general, very severe, and very bloody. At length, superiority of discipline carried the day from superiority of numbers. The conflict endured an hour and a half, and was terminated by General Greene's ordering a retreat, when he perceived that the enemy were on the point of encircling his troops."

This was a hard-fought action, and the exertions of the two rival generals, both in preparing for this action, and during the course of it, were never surpassed. Forgetful of every thing but the fortune of the day, they, on several occasions, mingled in the danger like common soldiers.

The loss sustained by the Americans in this battle, amounted, in killed and wounded, to only about four hundred; while, in its effect on the enemy, it was murderous; nearly one third of them, including many officers of distinction, were killed and wounded.

The result of this conflict, although technically a defeat, was virtually a victory on the part of General Greene. In its relation to his adversary, it placed him on higher ground than he had previously occupied; enabling him, immediately afterward, instead of retreating, to become the pursuing party. This is evidenced by his conduct soon after the action.

Not doubting that Lord Cornwallis would follow him, he retreated slowly, and in good order, from the field of battle, until attaining, at the distance of a few miles, an advantageous position, he again drew up his forces, determined to renew the contest on the arrival of his enemy. But his lordship was in no condition to pursue. Having, by past experience, not to be forgotten, learnt that his adversary was a Ulysses in wisdom, he now perceived that he was an Ajax in strength. Alike expert in every mode of warfare, and not to be vanquished either by stratagem or force, he found him too formidable to be again approached.

Influenced by these sentiments, Lord Cornwallis, instead of pursuing his foe, or even maintaining his ground, commenced his retreat, leaving behind him about seventy of his wounded, whom he recommended, in a letter written by himself, to the humanity and attention of the American chief.

Had General Greene been in a situation to pursue his lordship as soon as he commenced his retreat, the destruction of that officer and his army would have been inevitable. Some spot on the plains of Carolina would have witnessed the surrender that was reserved for Virginia; and the hero of the south would have won the laurels which shortly afterwards decorated the brow of the hero of the nation. But Greene's military stores were so far expended that he could not pursue, until he received a supply; and the delay, thus occasioned, gave time to the British commander to effect his escape.

Having received his supplies, Greene immediately pursued the enemy; but the advanced position of Lord Cornwallis, and the impracticable condition of the roads, frustrated every exertion that General Greene could make to compel the enemy to a second engagement: convinced of this, he halted to indulge his troops in that refreshment and repose which they so much needed.

Were we to indicate the period in the life of General Greene most strongly marked by the operations, and irradiated by the genius of a great commander, we would, without hesitation, select that which extends from the commencement of his retreat before Cornwallis, to the termination of his pursuit of him at this time. Perhaps a brighter era does not adorn the military career of any leader. It was in the course of it that he turned the current of adverse fortune consequent on the defeat of Gates, which he afterwards directed with such certain aim and irresistible force, as to keep the enemy from his numerous strong holds in the southern department, and contributed so pre-eminently to the speedy and felicitous issue of the war.

Having abandoned the pursuit of the British army, the general again found himself encircled with difficulties. Of the southern department of the Union, over which Greene's command extended, the enemy was in force in three large and important sections. Georgia and South Carolina were entirely in their possession; Lord Cornwallis had taken post in the maritime district of North Carolina, and part of Virginia was occupied by a powerful detachment of British troops, under the command of General Phillips. At a loss to determine in which of these points he should act in person, he consulted his officers, and found them greatly divided in opinion. He however resolved, in accordance to the views of Colonel Lee, that leaving his lordship, whose object evidently was the invasion of Virginia, to be met by the energies of that state, with such assistance as might arrive from the north, he should penetrate South Carolina, his army divided into two columns, attack and beat the enemy at their different posts, without permitting them to concentrate their forces, and thus recover that rich and important member of the Union.

An officer who had distinguished himself in the late action, not satisfied with the proposed plan of operations, asked General Greene, by way of remonstrance, "What will you do, sir, in case Lord Cornwallis throws himself in your rear, and cuts off your communication with Virginia?" "I will punish his temerity," replied the general with great pleasantness, "by ordering you to charge him as you did at the battle of Guilford. But never fear, sir; his lordship has too much good sense ever again to risk his safety so far from the sea-board. He has just escaped ruin, and he knows it, and I am greatly mistaken in his character as an officer, if he has not the capacity to profit by experience."

On the 7th of April, General Greene broke up his encampment, and with the main column of his army moving to the south, took position on Hobkirk's Hill, in front of Camden, the head-quarters of Lord Rawdon, now the commander-in-chief of the British forces in the south.

The strength of the British position, which was covered on the south and east side by a river and creek, and to the westward and northward by six redoubts, rendered it impracticable to carry it by storm with the small army Greene had, consisting of about seven hundred continentals, the militia having gone home. He therefore encamped at about a mile from the town, in order to prevent supplies from being brought in, and to take advantage of such favourable circumstances as might occur.

Lord Rawdon's situation was extremely delicate. Colonel Watson, whom he had some time before detached for the protection of the eastern frontiers, and to whom he had, on the intelligence of General Greene's intentions, sent orders to return to Camden, was so effectually watched by General Marion, that it was impossible for him to obey. His lordship's supplies were, moreover, very precarious; and should General Greene's reinforcements arrive, he might be so closely invested as to be at length obliged to surrender. In this dilemma, the best expedient that suggested itself, was a bold attack; for which purpose he armed every person with him capable of crrrying a musket, not excepting his musicians and drummers. He sallied out on the 25th of

April, and attacked General Greene in his camp. The defence was obstinate; and for some part of the engagement the advantage appeared to be in favour of America. Lieutenant-Colonel Washington, who commanded the cavalry, had at one time not less than two hundred British prisoners. However, by the misconduct of one of the American regiments, victory was snatched from General Greene, who was compelled to retreat. He lost in the action about two hundred killed, wounded and prisoners. Rawdon lost about two hundred and fifty-eight.

There was a great similarity between the consequences of the affair at Guilford, and those of this action. In the former, Lord Cornwallis was successful; but was afterward obliged to retreat two hundred miles from the scene of action, and for a time abandoned the grand object of penetrating to the northward. In the latter, Lord Rawdon had the honour of the field, but was shortly after reduced to the necessity of abandoning his post, and leaving behind him a number of sick and wounded.

The evacuation of Camden, with the vigilance of General Greene, and the several officers he employed, gave a new complexion to affairs in South Carolina, where the British ascendency declined more rapidly than it had been established. The numerous forts garrisoned by the enemy, fell, one after the other, into the hands of the Americans. Orangeburg, Motte, Watson, Georgetown, Granby, and others, Fort Ninety-Six excepted, were surrendered; and a very considerable number of prisoners of war, with military stores and artillery, were found in them.

On the 22d of May, General Greene sat down before Ninety-Six with the main part of his little army. The siege was carried on, for a considerable time, with great spirit; and the place was defended with equal bravery. At length the works were so far reduced that a surrender must have been made in a few days, when a reinforcement of three regiments from Europe arrived at Charleston, which enabled Lord Rawdon to proceed to relieve this important post. The superiority of the enemy's force reduced General Greene to the alternative of abandoning the siege altogether, or, previous to their arrival, of attempting the fort by storm. The latter was more agreeable to his enterprising spirit; and an attack was made on the morning of the 19th of June. He was repulsed with the loss of one hundred and fifty men. He raised the siege, and retreated over the Saluda.

Dr. Ramsay, speaking of the state of affairs about this period, says, "truly distressing was the situation of the American army; when in the grasp of victory, to be obliged to expose themselves to a hazardous assault, and afterward to abandon a siege. When they were nearly masters of the whole country, to be compelled to retreat to its extremity; and after subduing the greatest part of the force sent against them, to be under the necessity of encountering still greater reinforcements, when their remote situation precluded them from the hope of receiving a single recruit. In this gloomy situation there were not wanting persons who advised General Greene to leave the state, and retire with his remaining forces to Virginia. To arguments and suggestions of this kind he nobly replied, 'I will recover the country, or die in the attempt.' This distinguished officer, whose genius was most vigorous in those extremities when feeble minds abandon themselves to despair, adopted the only resource now left him, of avoiding an engagement until the British force should be divided."

Greene having, without loss, made good his passage over the rivers in front, Lord Rawdon, perceiving the futility of any further attempt to overtake him, abandoned the pursuit, and retreating to Ninety-Six, prepared for its evacuation. Thus did the policy of Greene, which is moral strength, compel the surrender of that fortress, although, from a want of physical strength, he failed to carry it by the sword.

No sooner had Lord Rawdon commenced his retrograde movement towards Ninety-Six, than General Greene changed his front and moved in the same direction. On the breaking up of the garrison of Ninety-Six, and the return of Lord Rawdon towards Charleston, which immediately ensued, the British army moved in two columns, at a considerable distance from each other. It was then that General Greene became, in reality, the pursuing party, exceedingly anxious to bring the enemy to battle. But this he was unable to accomplish until September.

September the 9th, General Greene having assembled about two thousand men, proceeded to attack the British, who, under the command of Colonel Stewart were posted at the Eutaw

Springs. The American force was drawn up in two lines; the first, composed of Carolina militia, was commanded by Generals Marion and Pickens, and Colonel de Malmedy. The second, which consisted of continental troops from North Carolina, Virginia, and Maryland, was commanded by General Sumpter, Lieutenant-Colonel Campbell, and Colonel Williams: Lieutenant-Colonel Lee, with his legion, covered the right flank; and Lieutenant-Colonel Henderson, with the state troops, covered the left. A corps de reserve was formed of the cavalry under Lieutenant-Colonel Washington, and the Delaware troops under Captain Kirkwood. As the Americans came forward to the attack, they fell in with some advanced parties of the enemy, at about two or three miles ahead of the main body. These being closely pursued, were driven back, and the action soon became general. The militia were at length forced to give way, but were bravely supported by the second line. In the hottest part of the engagement, General Greene ordered the Maryland and Virginia continentals to charge with trailed arms. This decided the fate of the day. "Nothing," says Dr. Ramsay, "could surpass the intrepidity of both officers and men on this occasion. They rushed on in good order, through a heavy cannonade and a shower of musketry, with such unshaken resolution that they bore down all before them." The British were broken, closely pursued, and upwards of five hundred of them were taken prisoners. They, however, made a fresh stand in a favourable position, in impenetrable shrubs and a picketed garden. Lieutenant-Colonel Washington, after having made every effort to dislodge them, was wounded and taken prisoner. Four six-pounders were brought forward to play upon them, but they fell into their hands; and the endeavours to drive them from their station being found impracticable, the Americans retired, leaving a very strong picket on the field of battle. Their loss was about five hundred; that of the British upwards of eleven hundred.

General Greene was honoured by Congress with a British standard and a gold medal, emblematical of the engagement, "for his wise, decisive, and magnanimous conduct in the action at Eutaw Springs, in which, with a force inferior in number to that of the enemy, he obtained a most signal victory."

In the evening of the succeeding day,

Colonel Stewart abandoned his post, and retreated towards Charleston, leaving behind upwards of seventy of his wounded, and a thousand stand of arms. He was pursued a considerable distance, but in vain.

In Dr. Caldwell's Memoirs of the Life of General Greene, we have the following interesting story as connected with the severe conflict at Eutaw Springs.

"Two young officers, bearing the same rank, met in personal combat. The American perceiving that the Briton had a decided superiority in the use of the sabre, and being himself of great activity and personal strength, almost gigantic, closed with his adversary, and made him his prisoner.

"Gentlemanly, generous, and high-minded, this event, added to a personal resemblance which they were observed to bear to each other, produced between these two youthful warriors an intimacy, which increased, in a short time, to a mutual attachment.

"Not long after the action, the American officer returning home on furlough, to settle some private business, obtained permission for his friend to accompany him.

"Travelling without attendants or guard,

they were both armed and well mounted. Part of their route lay through a settlement highly disaffected to the American cause.

"When in the midst of this, having, in consequence of a shower of rain, thrown around them their cloaks, which concealed their uniforms, they were suddenly encountered by a detachment of tories.

"The young American determined to die rather than become a prisoner, especially to men whom he held in abhorrence for disloyalty to their country, and the generous Briton resolved not to survive one by whom he had been distinguished and treated so kindly: they both together, with great spirit and self-possession, charged the royalists, having first made signals in their rear, as if directing others to follow them; and thus, without injury on either side, had the address and good fortune to put the party to flight.

"Arriving in safety at their place of destination, what was their surprise and augmented satisfaction on finding, from some questions proposed by the American officer's father, that they were first cousins!

"With increasing delight, the young Briton passed several weeks in the family of his kinsman, where the writer of this narrative saw him daily, and often listened, with the rapture of a child, to the checkered story of his military adventures.

"To heighten the occurrence, and render it more romantic, the American officer had a sister, beautiful and accomplished, whose heart soon felt for the gallant stranger more than the affection due to a cousin. The attachment was mutual.

"But here the adventure assumed a tragical cast. The youthful foreigner being exchanged, was summoned to return to his regiment. The message was fatal to his peace, but military honour demanded the sacrifice, and the lady, generous and high-minded as himself, would not be instrumental in dimming his laurels. The parting scene was a high-wrought picture of tenderness and sorrow. On taking leave the parties mutually bound themselves, by a solemn promise, to remain single a certain number of years, in the hope that an arrangement contemplated might again bring them together. A few weeks afterward, the lady expired under an attack of the small-pox. The fate of the officer we never learnt."

Judge Johnson in his Life of General Greene.

says, "At the battle of Eutaw Springs, Greene says, 'that hundreds of my men were naked as they were born.' Posterity will scarcely believe that the bare loins of many brave men who carried death into the enemy's ranks at the Eutaw, were galled by their cartouch-boxes, while a folded rag or a tuft of moss protected their shoulders from sustaining the same injury from the musket. Men of other times will inquire, by what magic was the army kept together? By what supernatural power was it made to fight?"

General Greene, in his letters to the secretary at war, says, "We have three hundred men without arms, and more than one thousand so naked that they can be put on duty only in cases of a desperate nature." Again he says, "Our difficulties are so numerous, and our wants so pressing, that I have not a moment's relief from the most painful anxieties. I have more embarrassments than it is proper to disclose to the world. Let it suffice to say that this part of the United States has had a narrow escape. *I have been seven months in the field without taking off my clothes.*"

The battle of Eutaw Springs being terminated, General Greene ordered the light troops under Lee and Marion to march circuitously, and gain a position in the British rear. But the British leader was so prompt in his measures, and so precipitate in his movements, that, leaving his sick and wounded behind him, he made good his retreat. The only injury he received in his flight was from Lee and Marion, who cut off part of his rear-guard, galled him in his flanks, killed several, and made a number of prisoners.

Such was the issue of the battle of Eutaw. Like that of every other fought by General Greene, it manifested in him judgment and sagacity of the highest order. Although he was repeatedly forced from the field, it may be truly said of that officer, that he never *lost* an action—the consequences, at least, being always in his favour. In no instance did he fail to reduce his enemy to a condition relatively much worse than that in which he met him, his own condition, of course, being relatively improved.

The battle of the Eutaw Springs was the last essay in arms, in which it was the fortune of General Greene to command, and was succeeded by the abandonment of the whole of South Carolina by the enemy, except Charleston

During the relaxation that followed, a dangerous plot was formed by some mutinous persons of the army, to deliver up their brave general to the British. The plot was discovered and defeated; the ringleader apprehended, tried, and shot, and twelve of the most guilty of his associates deserted to the enemy. To the honour of the American character, no native of the country was known to be concerned in this conspiracy. Foreigners alone were its projectors and abetters.

The surrender of Lord Cornwallis, whose enterprising spirit had been, by the British ministry, expected to repair the losses, and wipe away the disgrace which had been incurred through the inactivity and indolence of other generals, having convinced them of the impracticability of subjugating America, they discontinued offensive operations in every quarter. The happy period at length arrived, when, by the virtue and bravery of her sons, aided by the bounty of heaven, America compelled her invaders to acknowledge her independence. Then her armies quitted the tented field, and retired to cultivate the arts of peace and happiness. General Greene immediately withdrew from the south, and returned to the bosom of his native state.

The reception he there experienced was cordial and joyous. The authorities welcomed him home with congratulatory addresses, and the chief men of the place waited upon him at his dwelling, eager to testify their gratitude for his services, their admiration of his talents and virtues, and the pride with which they recognized him as a native of Rhode Island.

On the close of the war, the three southern states that had been the most essentially benefitted by his wisdom and valour, manifested at once their sense of justice, and their gratitude to General Greene, by liberal donations. South Carolina presented him with an estate valued at ten thousand pounds sterling; Georgia with an estate, a few miles from the city of Savannah, worth five thousand pounds; and North Carolina, with twenty-five thousand acres of land in the state of Tennessee.

Having spent about two years in his native state, in the adjustment of his private affairs, he sailed for Georgia in October, 1785, and settled with his family on his estate near Savannah. Engaging here in agricultural pursuits, he employed himself closely in arrangements for planting, exhibiting the fairest promise to become as eminent in the practice of the peaceful virtues as he had already shown himself in the occupation of war.

But it was the will of heaven that in this new sphere of action his course should be limited. The short period of seven months was destined to witness its commencement and its close.

Walking over his grounds, as was his custom, without his hat, on the afternoon of the 15th of June, 1786, the day being intensely hot, he was suddenly attacked with such a vertigo and prostration of strength, as to be unable to return to his house without assistance. The affection was what was denominated a "stroke of the sun." It was succeeded by fever, accompanied with stupor, delirium, and a disordered stomach. All efforts to subdue it proving fruitless, it terminated fatally on the 19th of the month.

Intelligence of the event being conveyed to Savannah, but one feeling pervaded the place. Sorrow was universal; and the whole town instinctively assumed the aspect of mourning. All business was suspended, the dwelling houses, stores, and shops, were closed, and the shipping in the harbour half-masted their colours.

On the following day, the body of the deceased being conveyed to the town, at the request of the inhabitants, was interred in a private cemetry with military honours; the magistrates of the place, and other public officers, the society of the Cincinnati, and the citizens generally, joined in the procession.*

In estimating the military character of General Greene, facts authorized the inference that he possessed a genius adapted by nature to military command. After resorting to arms, his attainment to rank was much more rapid than that of any other officer our country has produced; perhaps the most rapid that history records. These offices, so high in responsibility and honour, were conferred on him, not as matters of personal favour or family influence, nor yet through the instrumentality of political intrigue. They were rewards of pre-eminent merit, and tokens of recognised fitness for the highest functions of military service.

It is said, that on his very first appearance in the camp at Cambridge, from the ardour of

* General Greene left behind him a wife and five children.

his zeal, unremitted activity, and strict attention to every duty, he was pronounced by soldiers of distinction,* a man of real military genius.

"His knowledge," said General Knox to a distinguished citizen of South Carolina, "is intuitive. He came to us the rawest and most untutored being I ever met with; but in less than twelve months he was equal in military knowledge to any general officer in the army, and very superior to most of them." Even the enemy he conquered did homage to his pre-eminent talents for war. Tarlton, who had strong ground to know him, is reported to have pronounced him, on a public occasion, the most able and accomplished commander that America had produced.

When acting under the order of others, he never failed to discharge, to their satisfaction, the duties intrusted to him, however arduous. But it is the southern department of the Union that constitutes the theatre of his achievements and fame. It was there, where his views were unshackled and his genius free, that, by performing the part of a great captain, he erected for himself a monument of reputation, durable

* Colonel Pickering and others.

as history, lofty as victory and conquest could render it, and brightened by all that glory could bestow.

In compliment to his brilliant successes, the hivalric De la Luzerne, the minister of France, who, as a knight of Malta, must be considered as a competent judge of military merit, thus speaks of him: "Other generals subdue their enemies by the means with which their country or their sovereign furnished them, but Greene appears to subdue his enemy by his own means. He commenced his campaign without either an army, provisions, or military stores. He has asked for nothing since, and yet scarcely a post arrives from the south that does not bring intelligence of some new advantage gained over his foe. He conquers by magic. History furnishes no parallel to this."

On the 12th of August, of the year in which the general died, the Congress of the United States unanimously resolved, "That a monument be erected to the memory of the Honourable Nathaniel Greene, at the seat of the federal government, with the following inscription:

SACRED
to the Memory of the
HON. NATHANIEL GREENE,
who departed this Life
the 19th of June, MDCCLXXXVI,
late Major-General in the
Service of the U. S. and
Commander of the Army in the
Southern Department.
The United States, in Congress
assembled, in honour of
HIS PATRIOTISM, VALOUR, AND ABILITY,
have erected this
MONUMENT.

To the disgrace of the nation, no monument has been erected; nor, for the want of a headstone, can any one at present designate the spot where the relics of the *Hero of the South* lie interred.

DANIEL MORGAN,

BRIGADIER-GENERAL IN THE AMERICAN ARMY.

General Morgan was the creator of his own fortune. Born of poor, though honest parents, he enjoyed none of the advantages which result from wealth and early education. But his was a spirit that would not tamely yield to difficulties.

"He was born in New Jersey, where, from his poverty and low condition, he had been a day-labourer. To early education and breeding, therefore, he owed nothing. But for this deficiency his native sagacity and sound judgment, and his intercourse with the best society, made much amends in after life.

"Enterprising in his disposition, even now he removed to Virginia, in 1755, with a hope and expectation of improving his fortune. Here he continued, at first, his original business of day-labour; but exchanged it afterward for the employment of a wagoner.

"His military novitiate he served in the campaign under the unfortunate Braddock. The rank he bore is not precisely known. It must, however, have been humble; for, in consequence of imputed contumely towards a British officer, he was brought to the halbert, and received the inhuman punishment of five hundred lashes; or, according to his own statement, of four hundred and ninety-nine; for he always asserted that the drummer charged with the execution of the sentence, miscounted and jocularly added, 'That George the Third was still indebted to him one lash.' To the honour of Morgan he never practically remembered this savage treatment during the revolutionary war. Towards the British officers whom the fortune of battle placed within his power, his conduct was humane, mild, and gentlemanly.

"After his return from this campaign, so inordinately was he addicted to quarrels and boxing matches, that the village of Berrystown, in the county of Frederick, which constituted the chief theatre of his pugilistic exploits, received, from this circumstance, the name of Battletown.

"In these combats, although frequently overmatched in personal strength, he manifested the same unyielding spirit which characterized him afterward in his military career. When worsted by his antagonist, he would pause for a time, to recruit his strength, and then return to the contest, again and again, until he rarely failed to prove victorious.

"Equally marked was his invincibility of spirit in maturer age, when raised, by fortune and his own merit, to a higher and more honourable field of action. Defeat in battle he rarely experienced; but when he did, his retreat was sullen, stern, and dangerous.

"The commencement of the American revolution found Mr. Morgan married and cultivating a farm, which, by industry and economy, he had been enabled to purchase, in the county of Frederick.

"Placed at the head of a rifle company, raised in his neighbourhood in 1775, he marched immediately to the American head-quarters in Cambridge, near Boston.

"By order of the commander-in-chief, he soon afterward joined in the expedition against Quebec, and was made prisoner in the attempt on that fortress, where Arnold was wounded, and Montgomery fell.

"During the assault, his daring valour and persevering gallantry attracted the notice and admiration of the enemy.

"The assailing column to which he belonged

was led by Major Arnold. When that officer was wounded, and carried from the ground, Morgan threw himself into the lead, and, rushing forward, passed the first and second barriers. For a moment, victory appeared certain. But the fall of Montgomery closing the prospect, the assailants were repulsed, and the enterprise abandoned. During his captivity, Captain Morgan was treated with great kindness, and not a little distinction. He was repeatedly visited in confinement by a British officer of rank, who at length made an attempt on his patriotism and virtue, by offering him the commission and emoluments of colonel in the British army, on condition that he would desert the American and join the royal standard.

"Morgan rejected the proposal with scorn, and requested the courtly and corrupt negotiator 'never again to insult him in his misfortunes by an offer which plainly implied that he thought him a villian.' The officer withdrew, and did not again recur to the subject.

"On being exchanged, Morgan immediately rejoined the American army, and received, by the recommendation of General Washington, the command of a regiment.

"In the year 1777, he was placed at the

head of a select rifle corps, with which, in various instances, he acted on the enemy with terrible effect. His troops were considered the most dangerous in the American service. To confront them in the field was almost certain death to the British officers.

"On the occasion of the capture of Burgoyne, the exertions and services of Colonel Morgan and his riflemen were beyond all praise. Much of the glory of the achievement belonged to them. Yet so gross was the injustice of General Gates, that he did not even mention them in his official despatches. His reason for this was secret and dishonourable. Shortly after the surrender of Burgoyne, General Gates took occasion to hold with Morgan a private conversation. In the course of this he told him confidentially, that the main army was exceedingly dissatisfied with the conduct of General Washington; that the reputation of the commander-in-chief was rapidly declining; and that several officers of great worth threatened to resign, unless a change were produced in that department.

"Colonel Morgan fathoming in an instant the views of his commanding officer, sternly, and with honest indignation, replied, 'Sir, I have one favour to ask. Never again mention to me this hateful subject; under no other man but General Washington, as commander-in-chief, will I ever serve.'

"From that moment ceased the intimacy that had previously subsisted between him and General Gates.

"A few days afterward the general gave a dinner to the principal officers of the British, and some of those of the American army. Morgan was not invited. In the course of the evening, that officer found it necessary to call on General Gates, on official business. Being introduced into the dining-room, he spoke to the general, received his orders, and immediately withdrew, his name unannounced. Perceiving, from his dress, that he was of high rank, the British officers inquired his name. Being told that it was Colonel Morgan, commanding the rifle corps, they rose from the table, followed him into the yard, and introduced themselves to him, with many complimentary and flattering expressions, declaring that, on the day of action, they had very severely felt him in the field.

"In 1780, having obtained leave of absence from the army on account of the shattered condition of his health, he retired to his estate in the county of Frederick, and remained there until the appointment of General Gates to the command of the southern army.

"Being waited on by the latter, and requested to accompany him, he reminded him, in expressions marked by resentment, of the unworthy treatment he had formerly experienced from him, in return for the important services which, he did not hesitate to assert, he had rendered him in his operations against the army of General Burgoyne.

"Having received no acknowledgement, nor even civility, for aiding to decorate him with laurels in the north, he frankly declared that there were no considerations, except of a public nature, that could induce him to cooperate in his campaigns to the south. 'Motives of public good might influence him; because his country had a claim on him, in any quarter where he could promote her interest; but personal attachment must not be expected to exist where he had experienced nothing but neglect and injustice.'

"The two officers parted, mutually dissatisfied; the one, on account of past treatment; the other, of the recent interview.

"In the course of a few weeks afterward, Congress having promoted Colonel Morgan to the rank of brigadier-general by brevet, with a view to avail themselves of his services in the south, he proceeded without delay to join the army of General Gates. But he was prevented from serving any length of time under that officer, by his defeat near Camden, before his arrival, and his being soon afterward superseded in command by General Greene.

"Soon after taking command of the southern army, General Greene despatched General Morgan with four hundred continentals under Colonel Howard, Colonel Washington's corps of dragoons, and a few militia, amounting in all to about six hundred, to take position on the left of the British army, then lying at Winnsborough, under Lord Cornwallis, while he took post about seventy miles to his right. This judicious disposition excited his lordship's apprehensions for the safety of Ninety-Six and Augusta, British posts, which he considered as menaced by the movements of Morgan.

"Colonel Tarleton, with a strong detachment, amounting, in horse and foot, to near a thousand men, was immediately despatched by Cornwallis to the protection of Ninety-Six, with orders to bring General Morgan, if possible, to battle. To the ardent temper and chivalrous disposition of the British colonel this direction was perfectly congenial. Greatly superior in numbers, he advanced on Morgan with a menacing aspect, and compelled him, at first, to fall back rapidly. But the retreat of the American commander was not long continued. Irritated by pursuit, reinforced by a body of militia, and reposing great confidence in the spirit and firmness of his regular troops, he halted at the Cowpens, and determined to gratify his adversary in his eagerness for combat. This was on the night of the 16th of January, 1781. Early in the morning of the succeeding day Tarleton, being apprised of the situation of Morgan, pressed towards him with a redoubled rapidity, lest, by renewing his retreat, he should again elude him.

"But Morgan now had other thoughts than those of flight. Already had he, for several days, been at war with himself in relation to his conduct. Glorying in action, his spirit recoiled from the humiliation of retreat, and his resentment was roused by the insolence of pursuit. This mental conflict becoming more intolerable to him than disaster or death, his courage triumphed, perhaps, over his prudence, and he resolved on putting every thing to the hazard of the sword.

"By military men who have studied the subject, his disposition for battle is said to have been masterly. Two light parties of militia were advanced in front, with order to feel the enemy as they approached; and preserving a desultory, well aimed fire, as they fell back to the front line, to range with it, and renew the conflict. The main body of the militia composed this line, with General Pickens at its head. At a suitable distance in the rear of the first line, a second was stationed, composed of the continental infantry and two companies of Virginia militia, commanded by Colonel Howard. Washington's cavalry, reinforced with a company of mounted militia, armed with sabres, was held in reserve.

"Posting himself then in the line of the regulars, he waited in silence the advance of the enemy.

"Tarleton coming in sight, hastily formed his disposition for battle, and commenced the assault. Of this conflict, the following picture is from the pen of General Lee:

'The American light parties quickly yielded,

fell back, and arrayed with Pickens. The
enemy shouting, rushed forward upon the front
line, which retained its station, and poured in a
close fire; but continuing to advance with the
bayonet on our militia, they retired, and gained
with haste the second line. Here, with part
of the corps, Pickens took post on Howard's
right, and the rest fled to their horses, probably
with orders to remove them to a further
distance. Tarleton pushed forward, and was
received by his adversary with unshaken firm
ness. The contest became obstinate; and each
party, animated by the example of its leader,
nobly contended for victory. Our line maintained itself so firmly as to oblige the enemy
to order up his reserve. The advance of
M' Arthur reanimated the British line, which
again moved forward, and outstretching our
front, endangered Colonel Howard's right.
This officer instantly took measures to defend
his flank, by directing his right company to
change its front; but, mistaking this order, the
company fell back; upon which the line began to retire, and General Morgan directed it
to retreat to the cavalry. This manœuvre
being performed with precision, our flank became relieved, and the new position was

assumed with promptitude. Considering this retrograde movement the precursor of flight, the British line rushed on with impetuosity and disorder; but as it drew near, Howard faced about, and gave it a close and murderous fire. Stunned by this unexpected shock, the most advanced of the enemy recoiled in confusion. Howard seized the happy moment, and followed his advantage with the bayonet. This decisive step gave us the day. The reserve having been brought near the line, shared in the destruction of our fire, and presented no rallying point to the fugitives. A part of the enemy's cavalry having gained our rear, fell on that portion of the militia who had retired to their horses. Washington struck at them with his dragoons, and drove them before him. Thus, by a simultaneous effort, the infantry and cavalry of the enemy were routed. Morgan pressed home his success, and the pursuit became vigorous and general.'

" In this decisive battle we lost about seventy men, of whom twelve only were killed. The British infantry, with the exception of the baggage guard, were nearly all killed or taken. One hundred, including ten officers, were killed; twenty-three officers and five hundred privates were taken. The artillery, eight hundred muskets, two standards, thirty-five baggage wagons, and one hundred dragoon horses, fell into our possession."

In this battle, so glorious to the American arms, Tarleton had every advantage in point of ground, cavalry, and numbers, aided by two pieces of artillery.

Soon after this brilliant exploit, frequent attacks of the rheumatism compelled General Morgan to retire from the army, and he returned to his seat in Frederick, Virginia, where he continued in retirement until the insurrection in the western part of Pennsylvania, in 1794, when he was detached by the executive of Virginia, at the head of the militia quota of that state, to suppress it. This done, he returned into the bosom of his family, where he remained until death closed his earthly career, in 1799.

"There existed in the character of General Morgan a singular contradiction, which is worthy of notice.

"Although in battle no man was ever more prodigal of the exposure of his person to danger, or manifested a more deliberate disregard of death; yet, so strong was his love of life at other times, that he has been frequently heard to declare, 'he would agree to pass half his time as a galley-slave, rather than quit this world for another.'

"The following outline of his person and character is from the pen of a military friend, who knew him intimately:

'Brigadier-General Morgan was stout and active, six feet in height, strong, not too much encumbered with flesh, and was exactly fitted for the toils and pomp of war. His mind was discriminating and solid, but not comprehensive and combining. His manners plain and decorous, neither insinuating nor repulsive. His conversation grave, sententious, and considerate, unadorned, and uncaptivating. He reflected deeply, spoke little, and executed, with keen perseverance, whatever he undertook.

"A considerable time before his death, when the pressure of infirmity began to be heavy, he became seriously concerned about his future welfare. From that period, his chief solace lay in the study of the Scriptures, and in devotional exercises. He died in the belief of the truths of Christianity, and in full communion with the Presbyterian Church."

JOHN STARK,

Brigadier-General in the American Army.

General Stark was a native of New-Hampshire, and was born in Londonderry, August 17th, 1728. From his early youth he had been accustomed to the alarm of war, having lived in that part of the country which was continually subject to the incursions of the savages. While a child, he was captured by them, and adopted as one of their own; but after a few years was restored.

Arrived at manhood, his manners were plain, honest, and severe; excellently calculated for the benefit of society in the private walks of life; and as a courageous and heroic soldier, he is entitled to a high rank among those who have been crowned with unfading laurels, and to whom a large share of glory is justly due. He was captain of a company of rangers in the provincial service during the French war, in 1755.

From the commencement of the difficulties with the mother country, until the closing scene of the revolution, our country found in

General Stark one of its most resolute, independent, and persevering defenders. The first call of his country found him ready. When the report of Lexington battle reached him, he was engaged at work in his saw-mill: fired with indignation and a martial spirit, he immediately seized his musket, and with a band of heroes proceeded to Cambridge. The morning after his arrival, he received a colonel's commission, and availing himself of his own popularity, and the enthusiasm of the day, in two hours he enlisted eight hundred men. On the memorable 17th of June, at Breed's Hill, Colonel Stark, at the head of his backwoodsmen of New-Hampshire, poured on the enemy that deadly fire, from a sure aim, which effected such remarkable destruction in their ranks, and compelled them twice to retreat. During the whole of this dreadful conflict, Colonel Stark evinced that consummate bravery and intrepid zeal, which entitle his name to perpetual remembrance.

His spirit pervaded his native state, and excited them to the most patriotic efforts. The British General Burgoyne, in one of his letters, observes, "That the Hampshire Grants, almost unknown in the last war, now abound in the

most active and most rebellious race on the
continent, and hang like a gathering storm upon
my left."

Distinct from his efforts in rallying the
energies of his native state, he obtained great
credit in the active operations of the field. At
that gloomy period of the revolution, the retreat of Washington through New Jersey, in
1776, when the saviour of our country, apparently deserted of heaven and by his country,
with the few gallant spirits who gathered the
closer around him in that dark hour, precipi-
tately fled before an imperious and victorious
enemy—it was on this occasion that the persevering valour of Stark enrolled him among
the firm and resolute defenders of their country;
and, with them, entitles him to her unceasing
gratitude.

But as he fearlessly shared with Washington
the dark and gloomy night of defeat, so also
he participated with him in the joy of a bright
morning of victory and hope. In the successful enterprise against Trenton, Stark, then
a colonel, acted a conspicuous part, and covered
himself with glory. General Wilkinson, in
his memoirs, says, "I must not withhold due
praise from the dauntless Stark who dealt death

wherever he found resistance, and broke down all opposition before him."

Soon after this affair, Colonel Stark, from some supposed injustice toward him on the part of Congress, quitted the continental service, and returned to New Hampshire.

"When he was urged by the government of New Hampshire to take the command of their militia, he refused, unless he should be at liberty to serve or not, under a continental officer, as he should judge proper. It was not a time for debate, and it was known that the militia would follow wherever Stark would lead. The assembly therefore invested him with a separate command, and gave him orders to 'repair to Charlestown, on Connecticut River; there to consult with a committee of the New Hampshire Grants respecting his future operations, and the supply of his men with provisions; to take the command of the militia, and march into the Grants; to act in conjunction with the troops of that new state, or any other of the states, or of the United States, or separately, as it should appear expedient to him, for the protection of the people and the annoyance of the enemy.'"

Agreeably to his orders, Stark proceeded, in

a few days, to Charlestown; his men very
readily followed, and, as fast as they arrived,
he sent them forward to join the troops of
Vermont under Colonel Warner, who had
taken his situation at Manchester. At that
place he joined Warner with about eight
hundred men from New Hampshire, and found
another body of men from Vermont, who put
themselves under his command; and he was at
the head of fourteen hundred men. Most of
them had been in the two former campaigns,
and well officered; and were, in every respect,
a body of very good troops. Schuyler repeatedly urged Stark to join the troops under
his command, but he declined complying. He
was led to this conduct not only by the reasons
which have been mentioned, but by a difference
of opinion as to the best method of opposing
Burgoyne. Schuyler wished to collect all the
American troops in the front, to prevent Burgoyne from marching on to Albany. Stark
was of opinion that the surest way to check
Burgoyne was to have a body of men on his
rear, ready to fall upon him in that quarter,
whenever a favourable opportunity should present. The New England militia had not
formed a high opinion of Schuyler as

general; and Stark meant to keep himself in a situation in which he might embrace any favourable opportunity for action, either in conjunction with him, or otherwise; and with that view intended to hang on the rear of the British troops, and embrace the first opportunity which should present, to make an attack upon that quarter. But Stark assured Schuyler that he would join in any measure necessary to promote the public good, but wished to avoid any thing that was not consistent with his own honour; and if it was thought necessary, he would march to his camp. He wrote particularly, that he would lay aside all private resentment, when it appeared in opposition to the public good. But in the midst of these protestations he was watching for an opportunity to discover his courage and patriotism, by falling upon some part of Burgoyne's army.

While the American army was thus assuming a more respectable appearance, General Burgoyne was making very slow advances towards Albany. From the 28th of July to the 15th of August, the British army was continually employed in bringing forward batteaux, provisions, and ammuniton, from Fort George to the first navigable part of Hudson's River, a distance of not more than eighteen miles. The labour was excessive; the Europeans were but little acquainted with the methods of performing it to advantage, and the effect was in no degree equivalent to the expense of labour and time. With all the efforts that Burgoyne could make, encumbered with his artillery and baggage, his labours were inadequate to the purpose of supplying the army with provisions for its daily consumption, and the establishment of the necessary magazines. And after his utmost exertions for fifteen days, there were not above four day's provisions in the store, nor above ten batteaux in Hudson's River.

In such circumstances, the British general found that it would be impossible to procure sufficient supplies of provisions by the way of Fort George, and determined to replenish his own magazines at the expense of those of the Americans. Having received information that a large quantity of stores were laid up at Bennington, and guarded only by the militia, he formed the design of surprising that place; and was made to believe that as soon as a detachment of the royal army should appear in that quarter, it would receive effectual assistance from a large body of loyalists, who only waited for the appearance of a support, and would in that event come forward and aid the royal cause. Full of these expectations, he detached Colonel Baum, a German officer, with a select body of troops, to surprise the place. His force consisted of about five hundred regular troops, some Canadians, and more than one hundred Indians, with two light pieces of artillery. To facilitate their operations, and to be ready to take advantage of the success of the detachment, the royal army moved along the east bank of Hudson's River, and encamped nearly opposite to Saratoga; having, at the same time, thrown a bridge of rafts over the river, by which the army passed to that place. With a view to support Baum, if it should be found necessary, Lieutenant-Colonel Breyman's corps, consisting of the Brunswick grenadiers, light infantry, and chasseurs, were posted at Battenkill.

General Stark having received information that a party of Indians were at Cambridge, sent Lieutenant-Colonel Greg, on August the 13th, with a party of two hundred men, to stop their progress. Toward night he was informed by express that a large body of regulars was in the rear of the Indians, and advancing toward

Bennington. On this intelligence, Stark drew together his brigade, and the militia that were at hand, and sent on to Manchester, to Colonel Warner, to bring on his regiment; he sent expresses at the same time to the neighbouring militia, to join him with the utmost speed. On the morning of the 14th, he marched with his troops, and at the distance of seven miles he met Greg on the retreat, and the enemy within a mile of him. Stark drew up his troops in order of battle; but the enemy, coming in sight, halted upon a very advantageous piece of ground. Baum perceived the Americans were too strong to be attacked with his present force, and sent an express to Burgoyne with an account of his situation, and to have Breyman march immediately to support him. In the meantime small parties of the Americans kept up a skirmish with the enemy, killed and wounded thirty of them, with two of their Indian chiefs, without any loss to themselves. The ground the Americans had taken was unfavourable for a general action, and Stark retreated about a mile, and encamped. A council of war was held, and it was agreed to send two detachments upon the enemy's rear, while the rest of the troops should make an attack upon their front. The next day the weather was rainy, and though it prevented a general action, there were frequent skirmishes in small parties, which proved favourable and encouraging to the Americans.

On August the 16th, in the morning, Stark was joined by Colonel Symonds and a body of militia from Berkshire, and proceeded to attack the enemy, agreeably to the plan which had been concerted. Colonel Baum in the meantime had entrenched on an advantageous piece of ground near St. Koick's mills, on a branch of Hoosic River; and rendered his post as strong as his circumstances and situation would admit. Colonel Nichols was detached with two hundred men to the rear of his left, Colonel Herrick with three hundred men to the rear of his right; both were to join, and then make the attack. Colonels Hubbard and Stickney, with two hundred men, were ordered on the right, and one hundred were advanced towards the front, to draw the attention of the enemy that way. About three o'clock in the afternoon the troops had taken their station, and were ready to commence the action. While Nichols and Herrick were bringing their troops together, the Indians were alarmed at the prospect, and pushed off between the two corps; but received a fire as they were passing, by which three of them were killed and two wounded. Nichols then began the attack, and was followed by all the other divisions; those in the front immediately advanced, and in a few minutes the action became general. It lasted about two hours, and was like one continued peal of thunder. Baum made a brave defence; and the German dragoons, after they had expended their ammunition, led by their colonel, charged with their swords, but they were soon overpowered. Their works were carried on all sides, their two pieces of cannon were taken, Colonel Baum himself was mortally wounded and taken prisoner, and all his men, except a few who had escaped into the woods, were either killed or taken prisoners. Having completed the business by taking the whole party, the militia began to disperse and look out for plunder. But in a few minutes Stark received information that a large reinforcement was on their march, and within two miles of him. Fortunately at that moment Colonel Warner came up with his regiment from Manchester. This brave and experienced officer commanded a regiment of continental troops, which had been raised in Vermont. Mortified that he had not been in the former engagement, he instantly led on his men against Breyman, and began the second engagement. Stark collected the militia as soon as possible, and pushed on to his assistance. The action became general, and the battle continued obstinate on both sides till sunset, when the Germans were forced to give way, and were pursued till dark. They left their two field-pieces behind, and a considerable number were made prisoners. They retreated in the best manner they could, improving the advantages of the evening and night, to which alone their escape was ascribed.

In these actions the Americans took four brass field-pieces, twelve brass drums, two hundred and fifty dragoon swords, four ammunition wagons, and about seven hundred prisoners, with their arms and accoutrements. Two hundred and seven men were found dead upon the spot, the numbers of wounded were unknown. The loss of the Americans was but small; thirty were slain, and about forty were wounded. Stark was not a little pleased at having so fair an opportunity to vindicate his own conduct. He had now shown that no neglect from Congress had made him disaffected to the American cause, and that he had rendered a much more important service than he could have done by joining Schuyler, and remaining inactive in his camp. Congress embraced the opportunity to assign to him his rank; and though he had not given to them any account of his victory, or wrote to them at all upon the subject, on October the fourth they resolved, "That the thanks of Congress be presented to General Stark, of the New-Hampshire militia, and the officers and troops under his command, for their brave and successful attack upon, and signal victory over the enemy, in their lines at Bennington: and that Brigadier Stark be appointed a brigadier-general in the army of the United States." And never were thanks more deserved, or more wisely given to a military officer.

"In his official account of the affair, General Stark thus writes: 'It lasted two hours, *the hottest I ever saw in my life;* it represented one continued clap of thunder: however, the enemy were obliged to give way, and leave their field-pieces and all their baggage behind them: they were all environed within two breast-works with artillery; but our martial courage proved too strong for them. I then gave orders to rally again, in order to secure the victory; but in a few minutes was informed that there was a large reinforcement on their march, within two miles. Colonel Warner's regiment luckily coming up at the moment, renewed the attack with fresh vigour. I pushed forward as many of the men as I could to their assistance; the battle continued obstinate on both sides until sunset; the enemy was obliged to retreat; we pursued them till dark, and had day lasted an hour longer, should have taken the whole body of them.'

"On what small events does the popular humour and military success depend! The capture of one thousand Germans by General Washington, at Trenton, had served to wake up, and save the whole continent. The exploit of Stark at Bennington, operated with the same kind of influence, and produced a similar effect.

This victory was the first event that had proved encouraging to the Americans in the northern department, since the death of General Montgomery. Misfortune had succeeded misfortune, and defeat had followed defeat from that period till now. The present instance was the first in which victory had quitted the royal standard, or seemed even to be wavering. She was now found with the American arms, and the effect seemed, in fact, to be greater than the cause. It raised the spirit of the country to an uncommon degree of animation; and by showing the militia what they could perform, rendered them willing and desirous to turn out and try what fortunes would await their exertions. It had a still greater effect on the royal army. The British generals were surprised to hear that an enemy whom they had contemplated with no other feelings than those of contempt, should all at once wake up, and discover much of the spirit of heroism. To advance upon the mouth of cannon, to attack fortified lines, to carry strong entrenchments, were exploits which they supposed belonged exclusively to the armies of kings. To see a body of American militia, ill dressed, but little disciplined, without cannon, armed only with farmers' guns, without bayonets, and who had been accustomed to fly at their approach; that such men should force the entrenchments, capture the cannon, kill and make prisoners of a large body of the royal army, was a matter of indignation, astonishment and surprise."

"General Stark volunteered his services under General Gates at Saratoga, and assisted in the council which stipulated the surrender of General Burgoyne; nor did he relinquish his valuable services till he could greet his native country as an independent empire. General Stark was of the middle stature, not formed by nature to exhibit an erect soldierly mien. His manners were frank and unassuming, but he manifested a peculiar sort of eccentricity and negligence, which precluded all display of personal dignity, and seemed to place him among those of ordinary rank in life. His character, as a private citizen, was unblemished, and he was ever held in respect. For the last few years of his life, he enjoyed a pecuniary bounty from the government. He lived to the advanced age of ninety-three years, eight months, and twenty-four days, and died **May 8th, 1822.**"

HUGH MERCER,

MAJOR-GENERAL IN THE AMERICAN ARMY.

> To fight
> In a just cause, and for our country's glory,
> Is the best office of the best of men;
> And to decline when these motives urge,
> Is infamy beneath a coward's baseness.
> *Havard's Regulus.*

In the revolution which released our country from the domination of Great Britain, foreigners as well as native Americans, espoused the cause of the colonies. No examples are necessary to prove this:—we at once think of Steuben,—of Lafayette,—of Kosciusko—of the many who left their native land to strike a blow for freedom in the Western World. Numerous were the Britons, also, who joined the standard of patriotism, even though it was raised in opposition to the lion of their own banner. Instances of two of the most celebrated of these, both for their noble qualities and early deaths,—for they occurred during an early period of the contest,—we see in James Montgomery, and Hugh Mercer. The former we need not further mention in this place,—but of the latter we will give a brief sketch.

Hugh Mercer was born near Aberdeen in the north of Scotland, about the year 1723. He studied medicine, and as an assistant surgeon he was with the army of the Pretender, Charles Edward, at the field of Culloden. That battle was fought on the 16th April, 1746, and early in the year 1747, Mercer, fleeing from Scotland in consequence of his participation in the rebellion, landed at Philadelphia. Thirty years afterwards his corpse was interred in that place—and finally, on the 26th November 1840, his remains, with all the 'pride, pomp, and circumstance, of glorious war,' were removed from their first resting place, and buried in the beautiful cemetry of Laurel Hill, near the same city.

From Philadelphia Mercer proceeded to the frontier of Pennsylvania, and settled near the present village of Mercersburg, Franklin County. Here he remained engaged, it is believed, in farming occupations, until the commencement of the French and Indian war of 1755. After Braddock's defeat, the whole frontier of this province lay exposed to the attacks of the savages. The colonists were continually harassed by their incursions, and at last the Legislature raised a force of three hundred men, and gave the command to Colonel John Armstrong, under whom Mercer was appointed captain. The troops marched, in 1756, from Fort Shirley through a hostile country to the Alleghany river, and, unknown to the enemy, arrived at an Indian town called Kittaning, within twenty-five miles of Fort Du Quesne. At day-break the Americans attacked the place, and after a short action carried the town, and completely destroyed it. In this conflict Mercer was severely wounded in the right wrist and during the confusion which succeeded the taking of the Fort, he became separated from the rest of his company, and was obliged to set off alone, for the settlements. Becoming faint from loss of blood, and hearing the war-whoop of a body of Indians who approached, he secreted himself in the hollow trunk of a large tree. The savages came up, and stayed about the place some time, for the purpose of resting themselves, but soon continued their way. Mercer then pushed on, and, having reached the waters that emptied into the Potomac, he finally, after wandering in the woods for some weeks, arrived at Fort Cumberland.

In 1758, the provincial forces were reorganized, and placed in a more effective condition. Mercer was promoted to the rank of lieutenant-colonel, and accompanied General Forbes in his expedition to Fort Du Quesne. He was left with two hundred men in charge of the fort, and maintained it until he was relieved, notwithstanding the difficulties which attended it. Washington—with whom Mercer first became acquainted in this expedition—wrote to Governor Fauquier that the men left in the fort were "in such a miserable condition, having hardly rags to cover their nakedness, and exposed to the inclemency of the weather in this inclement season, that sickness, death and desertion, if they are not speedily supplied, must destroy them." As soon as he was relieved, Mercer left the army, and repaired to Fredericksburg, in Virginia, where he continued to practise his profession.

"The repose which the colonies enjoyed between the peace of 1763 and the beginning of the revolution, was short and restless. The young Nation lay, not in the slumber of exhaustion, but in the fitful sleep which the consciousness of a great futurity allows. It slept too with arms by its side, and there needed but the trumpet's feeblest note to arouse it to action. The involuntary concord of the Colonies at the outbreak of the Revolution is one of its most singular characteristics. It was a concord that transcended all mere political relations—it was beyond, and above all political union. It was the instinctive appreciation of common right, the quick sense of common injury. There seemed to be but one frame, and when the hand of tyranny was rudely laid on a single member, the whole system quivered beneath the contact, and braced itself to resistance."*

None of the colonies was more distinguished n the contest, for firm resistance to the arbitrary measures of the mother country, than were Massachusetts, Pennsylvania and Virginia. Hancock and Adams, Morris and Hopkinson, Henry and Jefferson,—all were untiring in their efforts to arouse their countrymen. Nor were these alone: other men, less celebrated in the annals of our country, perhaps, but yet equally patriotic, aided them. Of these Mercer was one. On the 25th of April 1775, he

* Reed's eulogy on General Mercer.

wrote to Washington informing him of an attack upon Williamsburg by some seamen from a British vessel, and of their removal of the powder from the magazine, by order of the Governor. He also said that the volunteer company of Fredericksburg intended to march in a few days to Williamsburg to secure the military stores yet remaining there. In June of the same year Washington was appointed Commander-in-chief, and on June 5th 1776, at the instance of Washington himself, Mercer was created Brigadier-General of the American troops.

The army was at New York when Mercer joined, and he remained with it constantly. The projected attack on Staten Island was confided to him—he was with the forces at White Plains—during the retreat through New Jersey,—and in short he continued in active service until his death.

The Americans had at last retired across the Delaware, but the gloomy appearance of their prospects increased. In Philadelphia "all able bodied men who were not conscientiously scrupulous about bearing arms," were ordered by General Putnam to "appear in the State House yard with their arms and accoutrements," that they might be sent to reinforce General Washington. With the assistance of these militia, it was resolved by the Commander-in-chief,—and the design was warmly seconded by Greene, Reed, and Mercer,—to attack the Hessian troops at Trenton. The result of this plan need not be here given; it is too well known to every reader of American history. General Washington immediately after the action recrossed the Delaware with his prisoners, and remained in his former position until the 29th of December, when he again entered New Jersey, and on the 2d of January met the main body of the British troops. The approach of darkness deferred the action, and during the night a council of the American officers was held to consider the means of rescuing themselves from the difficulties which surrounded them. In this state of affairs Mercer proposed the brilliant plan of ordering up the Philadelphia militia, and making a night march upon Princeton and Brunswick. It was agreed to without dissent and the troops were set in motion. General Mercer commanded the advanced party, and as day broke he observed a large body of British troops marching towards Trenton. He immediately proposed to the

Commander-in-chief to throw himself between this corps, and their reserve at Princeton, and thus bring on a general action,—and upon the consent of Washington he executed the movement. The Americans were however thrown into confusion at the death of Colonel Hazlet, and fell back. Mercer's horse was killed, but notwithstanding that he was alone, he refused to surrender and fought single handed with a British detachment which advanced towards him. The combat was too unequal, however, and he was beaten down by the butts of muskets and mortally wounded by bayonets. After the American troops had gained the day he was removed to a neighbouring house, and there expired, January 12th, 1777.

"On the 14th of January the remains of Mercer were brought to Philadelphia, and on the next day but one were interred in the grave from which they were removed to Laurel Hill November 26th 1840.

"There are aged men yet amongst us—so aged that before the brief remnant of this year expires the generation may cease to live—who remember the solemnity of that funeral. It was the Nation mourning for her first child. It was a people in sad amazement that a

gallant citizen had indeed died for them.
And when the ancient inhabitants of this city
thus gathered in throngs to bear the soldier's
mangled corpse to its place of rest, it was committed to the ground with the sacred service
which bade them look to the promised day
when "the earth and the sea shall give up their
dead." The grave thus solemnly closed
has been unsealed—affectionately, reverently,
piously.—But yet upon the solemnities of this
day, the reproach of a vain and profane pageant
may fasten, if the mouldering remains of the
dead can be placed in the midst of the living
without stirring every heart to its very centre."*

* Reed's eulogy. Delivered at Philadelphia November 26th, 1840, when the remains of Mercer were disinterred and again buried at Laurel Hill.

ETHAN ALLEN,

BRIGADIER-GENERAL IN THE AMERICAN ARMY.

General Allen was born in Salisbury, Connecticut, from whence, while he was yet young, his parents emigrated to Vermont. By this circumstance he was deprived of the advantages of an early education. But, although he never felt its genial influence, nature had endowed him with strong powers of mind; and when called to take the field, he showed himself an able leader, and an intrepid soldier.

At the commencement of the disturbances in Vermont, about the year 1770, he took a most active part in favour of the Green Mountain Boys, as the first settlers were then called, in opposition to the government of New York. Bold, enterprising, and ambitious, he undertook to direct the proceedings of the inhabitants, and wrote several pamphlets to display the supposed injustice and oppressive designs of the New York proceedings. The uncultivated roughness of his own temper and manners seems to have assisted him in giving a just description of the views and proceedings of speculating land-jobbers. His writings produced effects so hostile to the views of the state of New York, that an act of outlawry was passed against him, and five hundred guineas were offered for his apprehension. But his party was too numerous and faithful to permit him to be disturbed by any apprehensions for his safety. In all the struggles of the day he was successful, and proved a valuable friend to those whose cause he had espoused.

The news of the battle of Lexington determined Allen to engage on the side of his country, and inspired him with the desire of demonstrating his attachment to liberty by some bold exploit. While in this state of mind, a plan for taking Ticonderoga and Crown-Point by surprise, which was formed by several gentlemen in Connecticut, was communicated to him, and he readily engaged in the project. Receiving directions from the General Assembly of Connecticut, to raise the Green Mountain Boys and conduct the enterprise, he collected two hundred and thirty of the hardy settlers, and proceeded to Castleton. Here he was unexpectedly joined by Col. Arnold, who had been commissioned by the Massachusetts committee to raise four hundred men, and effect the same object which was now about to be accomplished. They reached the lake opposite Ticonderoga on the evening of the 9th of May, 1775. With the utmost difficulty boats were procured, and eighty-three men were landed near the garrison. Arnold now wished to assume the command, to lead on the men, and swore that he would go in himself the first. Allen swore that he should not. The dispute beginning to run high, some of the gentlemen present interposed, and it was agreed that both should go in together, Allen on the right hand, and Arnold on the left. The following is Allen's own account of the affair:—

"The first systematical and bloody attempt at Lexington, to enslave America, thoroughly electrified my mind, and fully determined me to take a part with my country. And while I was wishing for an opportunity to signalize myself in its behalf, directions were privately sent to me from the then colony, now state of Connecticut, to raise the Green Mountain Boys, and, if possible, with them to surprise and take the fortress of Ticonderoga. This enterprise I cheerfully undertook: and after first guarding all the several passes that led thither, to cut off all intelligence between the garrison and the country, made a forced march from Bennington, and arrived at the lake opposite Ticonderoga on the evening of the 9th day of May, 1775, with two hundred and thirty valiant Green-mountain Boys; and it was with the utmost difficulty that I procured boats to cross the lake. However, I landed eighty-three men near the garrison, and sent the boats back for the rear-guard, commanded by Col. Seth Warner; but the day began to dawn, and I found myself necessitated to attack the fort before the rear could cross the lake; and as it was viewed hazardous, I harangued the officers and soldiers in the manner following:—'Friends and fellow-soldiers, you have, for a number of years past, been a scourge and terror to arbitrary powers. Your valour has been famed abroad, and acknowledged, as appears by the advice and orders to me from the General Assembly of Connecticut, to surprise and take the garrison now before us. I now propose to advance before you, and in person conduct you through the wicket-gate; for we must this morning either quit our pretensions to valour, or possess ourselves of this fortress in a few minutes; and inasmuch as it is a desperate attempt, which none but the bravest of men dare undertake, I do not urge it on any contrary to his will. You that will undertake voluntarily, poise your firelock.'

"The men being at this time drawn up in three ranks, each poised his firelock. I ordered them to face to the right, and at the head of the centre file, marched them immediately to the wicket-gate aforesaid, where I found a sentry posted, who instantly snapped his fusee at me. I ran immediately towards him, and he retreated through the covered way into the parade within the garrison, gave a halloo, and ran under a bomb-proof. My party, wh followed me into the fort, I formed on th. parade in such a manner as to face the barracks, which faced each other. The garrison bein asleep, except the sentries, we gave three huzzas, which greatly surprised them. One of the sentries made a pass at one of my officers with a charged bayonet, and slightly wounded him. My first thought was to kill him with my sword, but in an instant I altered the design and fury of the blow to a slight cut on the side of the head; upon which he dropped his gun and asked quarters, which I readily granted him; and demanded the place were the commanding officer kept. He showed me a pair of stairs in the front of the garrison, which led up to a second story in said barracks, to which I immediately repaired, and ordered the commander, Captain Delaplace, to come forth instantly, or I would sacrifice the whole garrison; at which time the captain came immediately to the door with his breeches in his hand, when I ordered him to deliver to me the fort instantly; he asked me by what authority I demanded it. I answered him, 'In the name of the great Jehovah, and tł Continental Congress.' The authority of Congress being very little known at that time, he began to speak again; but I interrupted him, and with my drawn sword near his head, again demanded an immediate surrender of the garrison; with which he then complied, and ordered his men to be forthwith paraded without arms, as he had given up the garrison. In the meantime, some of my officers had given orders, and in consequence thereof, sundry of the barrack doors were beat down, and about one third of the garrison imprisoned, which consisted of said commander, a Lieutenant Feltham, a conductor of artillery, a gunner, two sergeants, and forty-four rank and file, about one hundred pieces of cannon, one thirteen inch mortar, and a number of swivels. This surprise was carried into execution in the gray of the morning of the 10th of May, 1775. The sun seemed to rise that morning with a superior lustre, and Ticonderoga and its dependencies smiled on its conquerors, who tossed about the flowing bowl, and wished success to Congress, and the liberty and freedom of America. Happy it was for me, at that time, that the future pages of the book of fate, which afterwards unfolded a miserable scene of two years and eight months' imprisonment, were hid from my view."

This brilliant exploit secured to Allen a high reputation for intrepid valour throughout the country. In the fall of 1775, he was sent twice into Canada to observe the dispositions of the people, and attach them, if possible, to the American cause. During one of these excursions, he made a rash and romantic attempt upon Montreal. He had been sent by General Montgomery, with a guard of eighty men, on a tour into the villages in the neighbourhood. On his return he was met by a Major Brown, who had been on the same business. It was agreed between them to make a descent upon the island of Montreal Allen was to cross the river, and land with his party a little north of the city; while Brown was to pass over a little to the south, with near two hundred men. Allen crossed the river in the night, as had been proposed; but, by some means, Brown and his party failed. Instead of returning, Allen, with great rashness, concluded to maintain his ground. General Carlton soon received intelligence of Allen's situation and the smallness of his numbers, and marched out against him with about forty regulars, and a considerable number of English, Canadians, and Indians, amounting, in the whole, to some hundreds. Allen attempted to defend himself, but it was to no purpose Being deserted by several of his men, and having fifteen killed, he, with thirty-eight of his men, were taken prisoners.

He was now kept for some time in irons, and was treated with the most rigorous and unsparing cruelty. From his narrative, it appears that the irons placed on him were uncommonly heavy, and so fastened, that he could not lie down otherwise than on his back. A chest was his seat by day and his bed by night. Soon after his capture, still loaded with irons, he was sent to England, being assured that the halter would be the reward of his rebellion when he arrived there. Finding that threats and menaces had no effect upon him, high command and a large tract of the conquered country, were afterward offered him, on condition that he would join the British. To the last he replied, "that he viewed their offer of conquered United States land to be similar to that which the devil offered to Jesus Christ: to give him all the kingdoms of the world, if he would fall down and worship him, when, at the same time, the poor devil had not one foot of land upon earth."

After his arrival, about the middle of December, he was lodged, for a short time, in Pendennis Castle, near Falmouth. On the 8th of January, 1776, he was put on board a frigate, and by a circuitous route again carried to Halifax. Here he remained closely confined in the jail from June to October, when he was removed to New-York. During the passage to this place, Captain Burke, a daring prisoner, proposed to kill the British captain, and seize the frigate; but Allen refused to engage in the plot, and was probably the means of saving the life of Captain Smith, who had treated him with kindness. He was kept at New-York about a year and a half, sometimes imprisoned, and sometimes permitted to be on parole. While here, he had an opportunity to observe the inhuman manner in which the American prisoners were treated. In one of the churches in which they were crowded, he saw seven lying dead at one time, and others biting pieces of chips from hunger. He calculated, that of the prisoners taken on Long-Island and at Fort-Washington, near two thousand perished by hunger and cold, or in consequence of diseases occasioned by the impurity of their prisons.

Colonel Allen was exchanged for a Colonel Campbell, May 6th, 1778, and after having repaired to head quarters, and offered his services to General Washington, in case his health should be restored, he returned to Vermont. His arrival on the evening of the last day of May gave his friends great joy, and it was announced by the discharge of cannon. As an expression of confidence in his patriotism and military talents, he was very soon appointed to the command of the state militia. His intrepidity, however, was never again brought to the test, though his patriotism was tried by an unsuccessful attempt of the British to bribe him to attempt a union of Vermont with Canada. He died suddenly on his estate, February 13th, 1789.

General Allen was brave, humane, and generous; yet his conduct does not seem to have been much influenced by considerations respecting that holy and merciful Being, whose character and whose commands are disclosed to us in the Scriptures. His notions with regard to religion were loose and absurd. He believed with Pythagoras, the heathen philosopher, that man, after death, would transmigrate into beasts, birds, fishes, reptiles, &c. and often informed his friends that he himself expected to live again in the form of a large white horse.

JOHN CADWALADER,

Brigadier-General in the American Army.

This zealous and inflexible friend of America was born in Philadelphia, 1742. He was distinguished for his intrepidity as a soldier, in upholding the cause of freedom during the most discouraging periods of danger and misfortune that America ever beheld.

At the dawn of the revolution, he commanded a corps of volunteers, designated as "*The silk stocking company*," of which nearly all the members were appointed to commissions in the line of the army. He afterwards was appointed colonel of one of the city battalions, and being thence promoted to the rank of brigadier-general, was intrusted with the command of the Pennsylvania troops, in the important operations of the winter campaign of 1776 and 1777. He acted with this command, as a volunteer, in the actions of Princeton, Brandywine, Germantown, and Monmouth, and on other occasions, and received the thanks of General Washington, whose confidence and regard he uniformly enjoyed.

The merits and services of General Cadwalader, induced Congress, early in 1778, to compliment him, by a unanimous vote, with the appointment of general of cavalry; which appointment he declined, under an impression that he could be more useful to his country in the sphere in which he had been acting.

He was strongly and ardently attached to General Washington, and his celebrated duel with General Conway arose from his spirited opposition to the intrigues of that officer to undermine the standing of the commander-in-chief. The following anecdote of the rencounter is related in the "Anecdotes of the Revolutionary War."

"The particulars of this duel, originating in the honourable feelings of General Cadwalader, indignant at the attempt of his adversary to injure the reputation of the commander-in-chief, by representing him as unqualified for the exalted station which he held, appears worthy of record. Nor ought the coolness observed on the occasion by the parties to be forgotten, as it evinces very strongly, that though imperious circumstances may compel men of nice feeling to meet, the dictates of honour may be satisfied without the smallest deviation from the most rigid rules of politeness. When arrived at the appointed rendezvous, General Cadwalader, accompanied by General Dickenson, of Pennsylvania, General Conway by Colonel Morgan, of Princeton, it was agreed upon by the seconds, that on the word being given, the principals might fire in their own time, and at discretion, either by an off-hand shot, or by taking a deliberate aim. The parties having declared themselves ready, the word was given to proceed. General Conway immediately raised his pistol, and fired with great composure, but without effect. General Cadwalader was about to do so, when a sudden gust of wind occurring, he kept his pistol down and remained tranquil. 'Why do you not fire, General Cadwalader?' exclaimed Conway. 'Because,' replied General Cadwalader, 'we came not here to trifle. Let the gale pass and I shall act my part.' 'You shall have a fair chance of performing it well,' rejoined Conway, and immediately presented a full front. General Cadwalader fired, and his ball entering the mouth of his antagonist, he fell directly forward on his face. Colonel Morgan running to his assistance, found the blood spouting from behind his neck, and lifting up the club of his hair, saw the ball drop from it. It had passed through his head, greatly to the derangement of his tongue and teeth, but did not inflict a mortal wound. As soon as the blood was sufficiently washed away to allow him to speak, General Conway, turning to his opponent, said, good humouredly, 'You fire, general, with much deliberation, and certainly with a great deal of effect.' The parties then parted, free from all resentment."

This patriotic and exemplary man died February 10th, 1786. In his private life he exemplified all the virtues that ennoble the character of man. His conduct was not marked with the least degree of malevolence or party spirit. Those who honestly differed from him in opinion, he always treated with singular tenderness. In sociability and cheerfulness of temper, honesty and goodness of heart, independence of spirit, and warmth of friendship, he had no superior. Never did any man die more lamented by his friends and neighbours; to his family and relations his death was a stroke still more severe.

THOMAS CONWAY,

MAJOR-GENERAL IN THE AMERICAN ARMY.

"This gentleman was born in Ireland, and went with his parents to France at the age of six years, and was, from his youth, educated to the profession of arms. He had obtained considerable reputation as a military officer, and as a man of sound understanding and judgment. He arrived from France with ample recommendations, and Congress appointed him a brigadier-general in May, 1777. He soon became conspicuously inimical to General Washington, and sought occasions to traduce his character. In this he found support from a faction in Congress, who were desirous that the commander-in-chief should be superseded. The Congress not long after elected General Conway to the office of inspector-general to our army, with the rank of Major-general, though he had insulted the commander-in-chief, and justified himself in doing so. This gave umbrage to the brigadiers over whom he was promoted, and they remonstrated to Congress against the proceeding, as implicating their honour and character. Conway, now smarting under the imputation of having instigated a hostile faction against the illustrious Washington, and being extremely unpopular among the officers in general, and finding his situation did not accord with his feelings and views, resigned his commission, without having commenced the duties of inspector. He was believed to be an unprincipled intriguer, and after his resignation, his calumny and detraction of the commander-in-chief, and the army generally, were exercised with unrestrained virulence and outrage.

No man was more zealously engaged in the scheme of elevating General Gates to the station of commander-in-chief. His vile insinuations and direct assertions in the public newspapers, and in private conversations, relative to the incapacity of Washington to conduct the operations of the army, received countenance from several members of Congress, who were induced to declare their want of confidence in him, and the affair assumed an aspect threatening the most disastrous consequences. Conway maintained a correspondence with General Gates on the subject, and in one of his letters he thus expresses himself: " Heaven has been determined to save your country, or a weak general and bad counsellors would have ruined it." He was himself at that time one of the counsellors against whom he so basely inveighs. Envy and malice ever are attendant on exalted genius and merit. But the delusion was of short continuance; the name of Washington proved unassailable, and the base intrigue of Conway recoiled with bitterness on his own head.

General Cadwalader, of Pennsylvania, indignant at the attempt to vilify the character of Washington, resolved to avenge himself on the aggressor in personal combat. The particulars of this meeting are given in the biography of General Cadwalader. General Conway, conceiving his wound to be mortal, and believing death to be near, acted honourably in addressing to General Washington, whom he had perfidiously slandered, the following letter of apology:

"*Philadelphia, Feb.* 23, 1778.

"Sir,—I find myself just able to hold my pen during a few minutes, and take this opportunity of expressing my sincere grief for having done, written, or said any thing disagreeable to your excellency. My career will soon be over, therefore, justice and truth prompt me to declare my last sentiments. You are, in my eyes, the great and good man. May you long enjoy the love, esteem, and veneration of these states, whose liberties you have asserted by your virtues.

 I am, with the greatest respect,
  Your Excellency's
   Most obedient and humble servant,
       THS. CONWAY.

WILLIAM RICHARDSON DAVIE,

Colonel-Commandant of the State Cavalry of North-Carolina.

Colonel Davie was born in the village of Egremont, in England, on the 20th of June, 1759. His father, visiting South Carolina soon after the peace of 1763, brought with him this son; and returning to England, confided him to the Rev. William Richardson, his maternal uncle: who becoming much attached to his nephew, not only took charge of his education, but adopted him as his son and heir. At the proper age, William was sent to an academy in North Carolina; from whence he was, after a few years, removed to the college of Nassau-Hall, in Princeton, New Jersey, then becoming the resort of most of the southern youth, under the auspices of the learned and respectable Dr. Witherspoon. Here he finished his education, graduating in the autumn of 1776, a year memorable in our military as well as civil annals.

Returning home, young Davie found himself shut out for a time from the army, as the commissions for the troops just levied had been issued. He went to Salisbury, where he commenced the study of law. The war continuing, contrary to the expectations which generally prevailed when it began, Davie could no longer resist the wish to plant himself among the defenders of his country. Inducing a worthy and popular friend, rather too old for military service, to raise a troop of dragoons, as the readiest mode of accomplishing his object, Davie obtained a lieutenancy in this troop. Without delay the captain joined the southern army, and soon afterward returned home on a furlough. The command of the troop devolving on Lieutenant Davie, it was, at his request, annexed to the legion of Count Pulaski, where Captain Davie continued, until promoted by Major-General Lincoln to the station of brigade-major of cavalry. In this office Davie served until the affair at Stono, devoting his leisure to the acquirement of professional knowledge, and rising fast in the esteem of the general and army. When Lincoln attempted to dislodge Lieutenant-Colonel Maitland from his entrenched camp on the Stono, Davie received a severe wound, and was removed from camp to the hospital in

Charleston, where he was confined five
months.

Soon after his recovery, he was empowered
by the government of North Carolina to raise
a small legionary corps, consisting of one troop
of dragoons and two companies of mounted
infantry; at the head of which he was placed
with the rank of major.

Quickly succeeding in completing his corps,
in whose equipment he expended the last
remaining shilling of an estate bequeathed to
him by his uncle, he took the field, and was
sedulously engaged in protecting the country
between Charlotte and Camden from the
enemy's predatory excursions. On the fatal
19th of August, he was hastening with his
corps to join the army, when he met our dis-
persed and flying troops. He nevertheless
continued to advance toward the conqueror;
and by his prudence, zeal, and vigilance, saved
a few of our wagons, and many of our strag-
glers. Acquainted with the movement of
Sumpter, and justly apprehending that he
would be destroyed unless speedily advised of
the defeat of Gates, he despatched immediately a courier to that officer, communicating
what had happened, performing, in the midst

of distress and confusion, the part of an experienced captain.

So much was his conduct respected by the government of North Carolina, that he was in the course of September promoted to the rank of colonel commandant of the cavalry of the state.

At the two gloomiest epochs of the southern war, soon after the fall of Charleston and the overthrow of Gates, it was the good fortune of Colonel Davie to be the first to shed a gleam through the surrounding darkness, and give hope to the country by the brilliancy of his exploits. In one instance, without loss or injury on his part, he entirely destroyed an escort of provisions, taking forty prisoners, with their horses and arms. In the other, under the immediate eye of a large British force, which was actually beating to arms to attack him, he routed a party stronger than his own, killing and wounding sixty of the enemy, and carrying off with him ninety-six horses and one hundred and twenty stand of arms.

When Lord Cornwallis entered Charlotte, a small village in North Carolina, Colonel Davie, at the head of his detachment, threw himself in his front, determined to give him a specimen of the firmness and gallantry with which the inhabitants of the place were prepared to dispute with his lordship their native soil.

Colonel Tarlton's legion formed the British van, led by Major Hanger, the commander himself being confined by sickness. When that celebrated corps had advanced near to the centre of the village, where the Americans were posted, Davie poured into it so destructive a fire, that it immediately wheeled and retired in disorder. Being rallied on the commons, and again led on to the charge, it received on the same spot another fire with similar effect.

Lord Cornwallis witnessing the confusion thus produced among his choicest troops, rode up in person, and in a tone of dissatisfaction upbraided the legion with unsoldierly conduct, reminding it of its former exploits and reputation.

Pressed on his flanks by the British infantry, Colonel Davie had now fallen back to a new and well selected position. To dislodge him from this, the legion cavalry advanced on him a third time, in rapid charge, in full view of their commander-in-chief, but in vain. Another fire from the American marksmen killed several of their officers, wounded Major Hanger, and repulsed them again with increased confusion.

The main body of the British being now within musket shot, the American leader abandoned the contest.

It was by strokes like these that he seriously crippled and intimidated his enemy, acquired an elevated standing in the estimation of his friends, and served very essentially the interest of freedom.

In this station he was found by General Greene, on assuming the command of the southern army; whose attention had been occupied from his entrance into North Carolina, in remedying the disorder in the quarter-master and commissary departments. To the first, Carrington had been called; and Davie was now induced to take upon himself the last, much as he preferred the station he then possessed. At the head of this department, Colonel Davie remained throughout the trying campaign which followed, contributing greatly by his talents, his zeal, his local knowledge, and his influence, to the maintenance of the difficult and successful operations which followed. While before Ninety-Six, Greene, foreseeing the difficulties again to be encountered in consequence of the accession of force to the enemy by the arrival of three regiments from Ireland, determined to send a confidential officer to the legislature of North Carolina, then in session, to represent to them his relative condition, and to urge their adoption of effectual measures without delay, for the collection of magazines of provisions and the reinforcement of the army. Colonel Davie was selected by Greene for this important mission, and immediately repaired to the seat of government, where he ably and faithfully exerted himself to give effect to the views of his general.

The effect of the capture of Cornwallis assuring the quick return of peace, Colonel Davie returned home, and resumed the profession with the practice of the law in the town of Halifax, on the Roanoke.

He was afterward governor of North Carolina, and one of our ambassadors to France at a very portentous conjuncture.

The war in the south was ennobled by great and signal instances of individual and partizan valour and enterprise. Scarcely do the most high drawn heroes of fiction surpass, in their darings and extraordinary achievements, many of the real ones of Pickens, Marion, Sumpter, and Davie, who figured in the southern states during the conflict of the revolution.

Colonel Davie, although younger by several years, possessed talents of a higher order, and was much more accomplished in education and manners, than either of his three competitors for fame. For the comeliness of his person, his martial air, his excellence in horsemanship and his consummate powers of field eloquence, he had scarcely an equal in the armies of his country. But his chief excellence lay in the magnanimity and generosity of his soul, his daring courage, his vigilance and address, and his unrelaxing activity and endurance of toil. If he was less frequently engaged in actual combat than either of his three compeers, it was not because he was inferior to either of them in enterprise or love of battle. His district being more interior, was, at first, less frequently invaded by British detachments. When, however, Lord Cornwallis ultimately advanced into that quarter, his scouts and foraging parties found in Colonel Davie and his brave associates, as formidable an enemy as they had ever encountered.

CHRISTOPHER GADSDEN,

Brigadier-General and Lieutenant-Governor of South Carolina.

This venerable patriot of the revolution was born in Charleston, about the year 1724. He was sent to England by his father, while a youth, where he was educated. At the age of sixteen he returned to Carolina, and finished his education in the counting-house of Mr. Lawrence, of Philadelphia.

General Gadsden had naturally a strong love for independence. He was born a republican. Under a well ordered government he was a good subject, but could not brook the encroachments of any man, or body of men, to entrench on his rights.

"As early as 1766," says Judge Johnson, "there was at least one man in South Carolina who foresaw and foretold the views of the British government, and explicitly urged his adherents to the resolution to resist even to death. General Gadsden, it is well known, always favoured the most decisive and energetic measures. He thought it folly to temporize, and insisted that cordial reconciliation, on honourable terms, was impossible. When the news of the repeal of the stamp-act arrived, and the whole community was in ecstacy at the event, he, on the contrary, received it with indignation, and privately convening a party of his friends, he harangued them at considerable length on the folly of relaxing their opposition and vigilance, or indulging the fallacious hope that Great-Britain would relinquish her designs or pretensions. He drew their attention to the preamble of the act, and forcibly pressed upon them the absurdity of rejoicing at an act that still asserted and maintained the absolute dominion over them. And then reviewing all the chances of succeeding in a struggle to break the fetters, when again imposed upon them, he pressed them to prepare their minds for the event. The address was received with silent but profound devotion; and with linked hands, the whole party pledged themselves to resist; a pledge that was faithfully redeemed when the hour of trial arrived."

"In June, 1775, when the Provincial Congress determined to raise troops, Gadsden, though absent on public duty at Philadelphia, was, without his consent or knowledge, elected colonel of the first regiment. For personal courage he was inferior to no man. In knowledge of the military art, he had several equals, and some superiors; but from the great confidence reposed in his patriotism, and the popularity of his name, he was put at the head of the new military establishment. He left Congress, and repaired to the camp in Carolina, declaring that 'wherever his country placed him, whether in the civil or military department; and if in the latter, whether as corporal or colonel, he would cheerfully serve to the utmost of his ability.'"

In the next year he was promoted by Congress to the rank of brigadier-general. He commanded at Fort-Johnson, when the fort on Sullivan's Island was attacked; and he was prepared to receive the enemy in their progress o Charleston. The repulse of the British prevented his coming into action. Their retreat elieved South Carolina from the pressure of war for two years. In this period, Gadsden resigned his military command, but continued o serve in the assembly and the privy council, and was very active in preparing for and endeavouring to repel the successive invasions of the state by the British in 1779 and 1780

He was the friend of every vigorous measure, and always ready to undertake the most laborious duties, and to put himself in the front of danger.

When Charleston surrendered by capitulation, he was lieutenant-governor, and paroled as such, and honourably kept his engagement. For the three months which followed, he was undisturbed; but on the defeat of Gates, in August, 1780, the British resolved that he and several others, who discovered no disposition to return to the condition of British subjects, should be sent out of the country. He was accordingly taken in his own house by a file of soldiers, and put on board a vessel in the harbour. He knew not why he was taken up, nor what was intended to be done with him, but supposed it was introductory to a trial for treason or rebellion, as the British gave out that the country was completely conquered.

He was soon joined by twenty-eight compatriots, who were also taken up on the same day.

He drew from his pocket half a dollar, and turning to his associates with a cheerful countenance, assured them that was all the money he had at his command. The conquerors sent him and his companions to St. Augustine, then a British garrison.

On their landing, limits of some extent were offered to them, on condition of their renewing the parole they had given in Charleston, " to do nothing injurious to the British interest." When this was tendered to General Gadsden, he replied, "That he had already given one, and honourably observed it; that, in violation of his rights as a prisoner under a capitulation, he had been sent from Charleston, and that, therefore, he saw no use in giving a second parole." The commanding officer replied, "He would enter into no arguments, but demanded an explicit answer whether he would or would not renew his parole." General Gadsden answered with that high-minded republican spirit which misfortunes could not keep down, "I will not. In God I put my trust, and fear no consequences." "Think better of it, sir," said the officer; "a second refusal will fix your destiny; a dungeon will be your future habitation." "Prepare it then," said the inflexible patriot, "I will give no parole, *so help me God*." He was instantly hurried off to the castle, and there confined for ten months in a small room, and in a state of complete separation from his fellow-prisoners, and in total ignorance of the advantages gained by his countrymen, but with most ample details of their defeats, and particularly of the sequestration of his estate with that of the other Carolina rebels.

After Andre's arrest, Colonel Glazier, the governor of the castle, sent to advise General Gadsden to prepare himself for the worst, intimating that as General Washington had been assured of retaliation if Andre was executed, it was not unlikely that he would be the person selected. To this message he magnanimously replied, "That he was always prepared to die for his country, and that he would rather ascend the scaffold than purchase with his life the dishonour of his country."

In the course of 1781, the victories of General Greene procured an equivalent for the release of all the prisoners belonging to South Carolina. Mr. Gadsden was discharged from close confinement, and rejoined his fellow-prisoners. The reciprocal congratulations on the change of circumstances, and on seeing each other after ten months separation, though in the same garrison, may be more easily conceived than expressed. They were all conveyed by water from St. Augustine to Philadelphia, and there delivered. On their arrival they were informed, for the first time, of the happy turn American affairs had taken subsequent to Gates' defeat. General Gadsden hastened back to Carolina to aid in recovering it from the British. He was elected a member of the assembly which met at Jacksonborough in 1782.

General Gadsden continued in the country throughout the year 1782, serving as one of the governor's council. On the 14th of December, 1782, he, with the American army and citizens, made their triumphant entry into Charleston in the rear of the evacuating British. In the first moment of his return, after an absence of more than two years, he had the pleasure of seeing the British fleet, upward of three hundred sail, in the act of departing from the port, and the capital, as well as the country, restored to its proper owners. Mr. Gadsden henceforward devoted himself to private pursuits, but occasionally served in the assembly, and with unspeakable delight in the two state conventions; the one for the ratification of the national constitution in 1788, and the other for revising the state constitution in 1790.

He survived his 81st year, generally enjoying good health, and at last died, more from the consequences of an accidental fall than the weight of disease, or decays of nature.

His opinions of lawyers were not favourable. He considered their pleadings as generally tending to obscure what was plain, and to make difficulties where there were none; and much more subservient to render their trade lucrative than to advance justice. He adhered to that clause of Mr. Locke's fundamental constitution, which makes it "a base and vile thing to plead for money or reward;" and wished that the lawyers, when necessary to justice, should be provided with salaries at the public expense, like the judges, that they might be saved from the shame of hiring their tongues to the first who offered or gave the largest fee. Of physicians he thought very little. He considered temperance and exercise superior to all their prescriptions, and that in most cases they rendered them altogether unnecessary. In many things he was particular. His passions were strong, and required all his religion and philosophy to curb them.

His patriotism was both disinterested and ardent. He declined all offices of profit, and through life refused to take the compensations annexed by law to such offices of trust as were conferred on him. His character was impressed with the hardihood of antiquity; and he possessed an erect, firm, intrepid mind, which was well calculated for buffeting with revolutionary storms."

HORATIO GATES,

Major-General in the American Army

General Gates was a native of England, and was born in the year 1728. He was educated to the military profession, and entered the British army at an early age, in the capacity of lieutenant, where he laid the foundation of his future military excellence. Without purchase he obtained the rank of major. He was aid to General Monckton at the capture of Martinico, and after the peace of Aix-la-Chapelle he was among the first troops which landed at Halifax under General Cornwallis. He was an officer in the army which accompanied the unfortunate Braddock in the expedition against Fort du Quesne, in the year 1755, and was shot through the body.

When peace was concluded, he purchased an estate in Virginia, where he resided until the commencement of the American war, in 1775. Having evinced his zeal and attachment to the violated rights of his adopted country, and sustaining a high military reputation, he was appointed by Congress adjutant-general, with the rank of brigadier, and he accompanied General Washington to the American camp at Cambridge, in July, 1775, where he was employed for some time in a subordinate, but highly useful, capacity.

In June, 1776, Gates was appointed to the command of the army of Canada, and on reaching Ticonderoga, he still claimed the command of it, though it was no longer in Canada, and was in the department of General Schuyler, a senior officer, who had rendered eminent services in that command. On representation to Congress, it was declared not to be their intention to place Gates over Schuyler, and it was recommended to these officers to endeavour to cooperate harmoniously. General Schuyler was, however, shortly after directed by Congress to resume the command of the northern department, and General Gates withdrew himself from it; after which he repaired to head-quarters, and joined the army under General Washington in Jersey.

Owing to the prevalent dissatisfaction with the conduct of General Schuyler in the evacuation of Ticonderoga, Gates was again directed to take command. He arrived about the 21st of August, and continued the exertions to restore the affairs of the department, which had been so much depressed by the losses consequent on the evacuation of Ticonderoga. It was fortunate for General Gates that the retreat from Ticonderoga had been conducted under other auspices than his, and that he took the command when the indefatigable, but unrequited labours of Schuyler, and the courage of Stark and his mountaineers, had already ensured the ultimate defeat of Burgoyne.

Burgoyne, after crossing the Hudson, advanced along its side, and encamped on the height, about two miles from Gates' camp, which was three miles above Stillwater. This movement was the subject of much discussion. Some charged it on the impetuosity of the general, and alleged that it was premature, before he was sure of aid from the royal forces posted in New York, but he pleaded the peremptory orders of his superiors. The rapid advance of Burgoyne, and especially his passage of the North River, added much to the impracticability of his future retreat, and made the ruin of his army in a great degree unavoidable. The Americans, elated with their successes at Bennington and Fort Schuyler, thought no more of retreating, but came out to meet the advancing British, and engaged them with firmness and resolution.

The attack began a little before mid-day, September 19th, between the scouting parties of the two armies. The commanders of both sides supported and reinforced their respective parties. The conflict, though severe, was only partial for an hour and a half; but after a short pause, it became general, and continued for three hours without any intermission. A constant blaze of fire was kept up, and both armies seemed determined on death or victory. The Americans and British alternately drove, and were driven by each other. The British artillery fell into our possession at every charge, but we could neither turn the pieces upon the enemy nor bring them off, so sudden were the alternate advantages. It was a gallant conflict, in which death, by familiarity, lost his terrors; and such was the order of the Americans, that, as General Wilkinson states, the wounded men, after having their wounds dressed, in many instances returned again into the battle. Men, and particularly officers, dropped every moment, and on every side. Several of the Americans placed themselves on high trees, and as often as they could distinguish an officer's uniform, took him off by deliberately aiming at his person. Few actions have been characterized by more obstinacy in attack or defence. The British repeatedly tried their bayonets, but without their usual success in the use of that weapon.

The British lost upwards of five hundred men, including their killed, wounded, and prisoners. The Americans, inclusive of the missing, lost three hundred and nineteen. Thirty-six out of forty-eight British artillerists were killed or wounded. The 62d British regiment, which was five hundred strong when it left Canada, was reduced to sixty men, and four or five officers. In this engagement General Gates, assisted by Generals Lincoln and Arnold, commanded the American army, and General Burgoyne was at the head of his army, and Generals Phillips, Reidesel, and Frazer, with their respective commands, were actively engaged.

This battle was fought by the general concert and zealous cooperation of the corps engaged, and was sustained more by individual courage than military discipline. General Arnold, who afterwards traitorously deserted his country, behaved with the most undaunted courage, leading on the troops, and encouraging them by his personal efforts and daring exposure. The gallant Colonel Morgan obtained immortal honour on this day. Lieutenant-Colonel Brooks, with the eighth Massachusetts' regiment, remained in the field till about eleven o'clock, and was the last who retired. Major Hull commanded a detachment of three hundred men, who fought with such signal ardour that more than half of them were killed. The whole number of Americans engaged in this action was about two thousand five hundred; the remainder of the army, from its unfavourable situation, took little or no part in the action.

Each army claimed the victory, and each believed himself to have beaten, with only part of its force, nearly the whole of the enemy. The advantage, however, was decidedly in favour of the Americans. In every quarter they had been the assailants, and after an encounter of several hours they had not lost a single inch of ground.

General Gates, whose numbers increased daily, remained on his old ground. His right, which extended to the river, had been rendered unassailable, and he used great industry to strengthen his left.

Both armies retained their position until the 7th of October; Burgoyne, in the hope of being relieved by Sir Henry Clinton; and Gates, in he confidence of growing stronger every day and of rendering the destruction of his enemy more certain. But receiving no further in telligence from Sir Henry, the British general determined to make one more trial of strength with his adversary. The following account of the brilliant affair of the 7th of October, 1777, is given in Thacher's Military Journal:—

"I am fortunate enough to obtain from our officers, a particular account of the glorious event of the 7th instant. The advanced parties of the two armies came into contact about three o'clock on Tuesday afternoon, and immediately displayed their hostile attitude. The Americans soon approached the royal army, and each party in defiance awaited the deadly blow. The gallant Colonel Morgan, at the head of his famous rifle corps, and Major Dearborn, leading a detachment of infantry, commenced the action, and rushed courageously on the British grenadiers, commanded by Major Ackland; and the furious attack was most firmly resisted. In all parts of the field the conflict became extremely arduous and obstinate; an unconquerable spirit on each side disdaining to yield the palm of victory. Death appeared to have lost his terrors; breaches in the ranks were no sooner made than supplied by fresh combatants, awaiting a similar fate. At length the Americans press forward with renewed strength and ardour, and compel the whole British line, commanded by Burgoyne himself, to yield to their deadly fire, and they retreat in disorder. The German troops remain firmly posted at their lines; these were now boldly assaulted by Brigadier-General Learned, and Lieutenant-Colonel Brooks, at the head of their respective commands, with such intrepidity, that the works were carried, and their brave commander, Lieutenant-Colonel Breyman, was slain. The Germans were pursued to their encampment, which, with all the equipage of the brigade, fell into our hands. Colonel Cilley, of General Poor's brigade, having acquitted himself honourably, was seen astride on a brass field-piece, exulting in the capture. Major Hull, of the Massachusetts line, was among those who so bravely stormed the enemy's entrenchment, and acted a conspicuous part. General Arnold, in consequence of a serious misunderstanding with General Gates, was not vested with any command, by which he was exceedingly chagrined and irritated. He entered the field, however, and his conduct was marked with intemperate rashness; flourishing his sword, and animating the troops, he struck an officer on the head without cause, and gave him a considerable wound. He exposed himself to every danger, and, with a small party of riflemen, rushed into the rear of the enemy, where he received a ball which fractured his leg, and his horse was killed under him. Nightfall put a stop to our brilliant career, though the victory was most decisive; and it is with pride and exultation that we recount the triumph of American bravery. Besides Lieutenant-Colonel Breyman slain, General Frazer, one of the most valuable officers in the British service, was mortally wounded, and survived but a few hours. Frazer was the soul of the British army, and was just changing the disposition of a part of the troops to repel a strong impression which the Americans had made, and were still making, on the British right, when Morgan called together two or three of his best marksmen, and pointing to Frazer, said, 'Do you see that gallant officer? that is General Frazer—I respect and honour him; but it is necessary he should die.' This was enough. Frazer immediately received his mortal wound, and was carried off the field. Sir Francis Clark, aid-de-camp to General Burgoyne, was brought into our camp with a mortal wound, and Major Ackland, who commanded the British grenadiers, was wounded through both legs, and is our prisoner. Several other officers, and about two hundred privates, are prisoners in our hands, with nine pieces of cannon, and a considerable supply of ammunition, which was much wanted for our troops. The loss on our side is supposed not to exceed thirty killed, and one hundred wounded, in obtaining this signal victory."

The position of the British army, after the action of the 7th, was so dangerous, that an immediate and total change of position became necessary, and Burgoyne took immediate measures to regain his former camp at Saratoga. There he arrived with little molestation from his adversary. His provisions being now reduced to the supply of a few days, the transports of artillery and baggage towards

Canada being rendered impracticable by the judicious measures of his adversary, the British general resolved upon a rapid retreat, merely with what the soldiers could carry. On examination, however, it was found that they were deprived even of this resource, as the passes through which their route lay, were so strongly guarded, that nothing but artillery could clear them. In this desperate situation a parley took place, and on the 17th of October the whole army surrendered to General Gates.

The prize obtained consisted of more than five thousand prisoners, forty-two pieces of brass ordnance, seven thousand muskets, clothing for seven thousand men, with a great quantity of tents, and other military stores.

Soon after the convention was signed, the Americans marched into their lines, and were kept there until the royal army had deposited their arms at the place appointed. The delicacy with which this business was conducted, reflected honour on the American general. Nor did the politeness of Gates end here. Every circumstance was withheld that could constitute a triumph in the American army. The captive general was received by his conqueror with respect and kindness. A number of the principal officers of both armies met at General Gates' quarters, and for a while seemed to forget, in social and convivial pleasures, that they had been enemies.

General Wilkinson gives the following account of the meeting between General Burgoyne and General Gates:

"General Gates, advised of Burgoyne's approach, met him at the head of his camp, Burgoyne in a rich royal uniform, and Gates in a plain blue frock. When they had approached nearly within sword's length, they reined up and halted. I then named the gentleman, and General Burgoyne, raising his hat most gracefully, said, 'The fortune of war, General Gates, has made me your prisoner;' to which the conqueror, returning a courtly salute, promptly replied, 'I shall always be ready to bear testimony that it has not been through any fault of your excellency.'"

The thanks of Congress were voted to General Gates and his army; and a medal of gold, in commemoration of this great event, was ordered to be struck, to be presented to him by the president, in the name of the United States.

It was not long after that the wonderful discovery was supposed to be made, that the illustrious Washington was incompetent to the task of conducting the operations of the American army, and that General Gates, if elevated to the chief command, would speedily meliorate the condition of our affairs. There were those who imputed to General Gates himself a principal agency in the affair, which, however, he promptly disavowed. But certain it is, that a private correspondence was maintained between him and the intriguing General Conway, in which the measures pursued by General Washington are criticised and reprobated; and in one of Conway's letters, he pointedly ascribes our want of success to a weak general and bad counsellors. Genera Gates, on finding that General Washington had been apprised of the correspondence, addressed his excellency, requesting that he would disclose the name of his informant; and in violation of the rules of decorum, he addressed the commander-in-chief on a subject of extreme delicacy, in an open letter transmitted to the president of Congress. General Washington, however, did not hesitate to disclose the name and circumstances which brought the affair to light. General Gates, then, with inexcusable disingenuousness, attempted to vindicate the conduct of Conway, and to deny that the letter contained the reprehensible expressions in question, but utterly refused to produce the original letter. This subject, however, was so ably and candidly discussed by General Washington, as to cover his adversary with shame and humiliation. It was thought inexcusable in Gates, that he neglected to communicate to the commander-in-chief an account of so important an event as the capture of the British army at Saratoga, but left his excellency to obtain the information by common report.

Dr. Thacher, in his Military Journal, relates the following anecdote: "Mr. T——, an ensign in our regiment, has, for some time, discovered symptoms of mental derangement. Yesterday he intruded himself at General Gates' head-quarters, and after some amusing conversation, he put himself in the attitude of devotion, and prayed that God would pardon General Gates for endeavouring to supersede that god-like man, Washington. The general appeared to be much disturbed, and directed Mr. Pierce, his aid-de-camp, to take him away."

On the 13th of June, 1780, General Gates was appointed to the chief command of the southern army. Rich in fame from the fields of Saratoga, he hastened to execute the high and important trust; and the arrival of an officer so exalted in reputation, had an immediate and happy effect on the spirits of the soldiery and the hopes of the people. It was anticipated that he who had humbled Great Britain on the heights of the Hudson, and liberated New York from a formidable invasion, would prove no less successful in the south, and become the deliverer of Carolina and Georgia from lawless rapine and military rule. But anticipations were vain, and the best founded hopes were blighted! In the first and only encounter which he had with Lord Cornwallis, at Camden, August 15th, he suffered a total defeat, and was obliged to fly from the enemy for personal safety.*

Proudly calculating on the weight of his name, and too confident in his own superiority, he slighted the counsel which he ought to have respected, and hurrying impetuously into the

---

* When the appointment of General Gates to the chief command of the southern army was announced, General Lee remarked, that "*his northern laurels would soon be exchanged for southern willows.*"

field of battle, his tide of popularity ebbed as fast at Camden as it had flowed at Saratoga.

It would be great injustice, however, to attribute the misfortune altogether to the commander, under his peculiar circumstances. A large proportion of his force consisted of raw militia, who were panic-struck, and fled at the first fire; their rout was absolute and irretrievable. In vain did Gates attempt to rally them That their speed might be the greater, they threw away their arms and accoutrements, and dashed into the woods and swamps for safety. A rout more perfectly wild and disorderly, or marked with greater consternation and dismay, was never witnessed. Honour, manhood, country, home, every recollection sacred to the feelings of the soldier and the soul of the brave, was merged in an ignominious love of life.

But from the moment General Gates assumed the command in the south, his former judgment and fortune seemed to forsake him. He was anxious to come to action immediately, and to terminate the war by a few bold and energetic measures; and two days after his arrival in camp, he began his march to meet the enemy, without properly estimating his force.

The active spirits of the place being roused

and encouraged by the presence of a considerable army, and daily flocking to the standard of their country, General Gates, by a delay of action, had much to gain in point of numbers. To the prospects of the enemy, on the contrary, delay would have been ruinous. To them there was no alternative but immediate battle and victory, or immediate retreat. Such, however, was the nature of the country, and the distance and relative position of the two armies, that to compel the Americans to action was impossible. The imprudence of the American general in hazarding an engagement at this time, is further manifested by the fact, that in troops on whose firmness he could safely rely, he was greatly inferior to his foe, they amounting to sixteen hundred veteran and highly disciplined regulars, and he having less than a thousand continentals.

General Gates having retreated to Salisbury, and thence to Hillsborough, he there succeeded in collecting around him the fragments of an army. Being soon after reinforced by several small bodies of regulars and militia, he again advanced towards the south, and took post in Charlotte. Here he continued in command until the 5th day of October, fifty days after his defeat at Camden, when Congress passed a resolution requiring the commander-in-chief to order a court of inquiry on his conduct, as commander of the southern army, and to appoint some other officer to that command. The inquiry resulted in his acquittal; and it was the general opinion that he was not treated by Congress with that delicacy, or indeed gratitude, that was due to an officer of his acknowledged merit. He, however, received the order of his supersedure and suspension, and resigned the command to General Greene with becoming dignity, as is manifested, much to his credit, in the following order:

"*Head-quarters, Charlotte, 3d Dec*, 1780. Parole, Springfield—countersign, Greene.

"The honourable Major-General Greene, who arrived yesterday afternoon in Charlotte, being appointed by his excellency General Washington, with the approbation of the honourable Congress, to the command of the southern army, all orders will, for the future, issue from him, and all reports are to be made to him.

"General Gates returns his sincere and grateful thanks to the southern army for their perseverance, fortitude, and patient endurance of all the hardships and sufferings they have undergone while under his command. He anxiously hopes their misfortunes will cease therewith, and that victory, and the glorious advantages of it, may be the future portion of the southern army."

General Greene had always been, and continued to be, the firm advocate of the reputation of General Gates, particularly if he heard it assailed with asperity; and still believed and asserted, that if there was any mistake in the conduct of Gates, it was in hazarding an action at all against such superior force; and when informed of his appointment to supersede him, declared his confidence in his military talents, and his willingness "to serve under him."

General Gates was reinstated in his military command in the main army, in 1782; but the great scenes of war were now passed, and he could only participate in the painful scene of a final separation.

In the midst of his misfortune, General Gates was called to mourn the afflictive dispensation of Providence, in the death of his only son. Major Garden, in his excellent publication, has recorded the following affecting anecdote, which he received from Dr. William Reed:

"Having occasion to call on General Gates, relative to the business of the department under my immediate charge, I found him traversing the apartment which he occupied, under the influence of high excitement; his agitation was excessive—every feature of his countenance, every gesture betrayed it. Official despatches, informing him that he was superseded, and that the command of the southern army had been transferred to General Greene, had just been received and perused by him. His countenance, however, betrayed no expression of irritation or resentment; it was sensibility alone that caused his emotion. An open letter, which he held in his hand, was often raised to his lips, and kissed with devotion, while the exclamation repeatedly escaped them—'Great man! Noble, generous procedure!' When the tumult of his mind had subsided, and his thoughts found utterance, he, with strong expression of feeling, exclaimed, 'I have received this day a communication from the commander-in-chief, which has conveyed more consolation to my bosom, more ineffable delight to my heart, than I had believed it possible for it ever to have felt again. With affectionate tenderness he sympathizes with me in my domestic misfortunes, and condoles with me on the loss I have sustained by the recent death of an only son; and then with peculiar delicacy, lamenting my misfortune in battle, assures me that his confidence in my zeal and capacity is so little impaired, that the command of the right wing of the army will be bestowed on me so soon as I can make it convenient to join him.'"

After the peace he retired to his farm in Berkley county, Virginia, where he remained until the year 1790, when he went to reside in New York, having first emancipated his slaves, and made a pecuniary provision for such as were not able to provide for themselves. Some of them would not leave him, but continued in his family.

On his arrival at New York, the freedom of the city was presented to him. In 1800 he accepted a seat in the legislature, but he retained it no longer than he conceived his services might be useful to the cause of liberty, which he never abandoned.

His political opinions did not separate him from many respectable citizens, whose views differed widely from his own. He had a handsome person, and was gentlemanly in his manners, remarkably courteous to all, and gave indisputable marks of a social, amiable, and benevolent disposition. A few weeks before his death he closed a letter to a friend in the following words:—"I am very weak, and have evident signs of an approaching dissolution. But I have lived long enough, since I have to see a mighty people animated with a spirit to be free, and governed by transcendent abilities and honour." He died without posterity, at his abode near New York, on the 10th day of April, 1806, aged seventy-eight years.

NATHAN HALE,

Captain in the American Army.

After the unfortunate engagement on Long Island, General Washington called a council of war, who determined on an immediate retreat to New York. The intention was prudently concealed from the army, who knew not whither they were going, but imagined it was to attack the enemy. The field artillery, tents, baggage, and about nine thousand men, were conveyed to the city of New York, over the East River, more than a mile wide, in less than thirteen hours, and without the knowledge of the British, though not six hundred yards distant. Providence in a remarkable manner favoured the retreating army. The wind, which seemed to prevent the troops getting over at the appointed hour, afterward shifted to their wishes.

Perhaps the fate of America was never suspended by a more brittle thread than previously to this memorable retreat. A spectacle is here presented of an army destined for the defence of a great continent, driven to the narrow borders of an island, with a victorious army double its number in front, with navigable waters in its rear; constantly liable to have its communication cut off by the enemy's navy, and every moment exposed to an attack. The presence of mind which animated the commander-in-chief in this critical situation, the prudence with which all the necessary measures were executed, redounded as much or more to his honour than the most brilliant victories. An army, to which America looked for safety, preserved; a general who was considered as an host himself, saved for the future necessities of his country. Had not, however, the circumstances of the night, of the wind and weather, been favourable, the plan, however well concerted, must have been defeated. To a good Providence, therefore, are the people of America indebted for the complete success of an enterprise so important in its consequences.

This retreat left the British in complete possession of Long Island. What would be their future operations remained uncertain. To obtain information of their situation, their strength, and future movements, was of high importance. For this purpose, General Washington applied to Colonel Knowlton, who commanded a regiment of light infantry, which formed the rear of the American army, and desired him to adopt some mode of gaining the necessary information. Colonel Knowlton communicated this request to Captain NATHAN HALE, of Connecticut, who was a captain in his regiment.

This young officer, animated by a sense of duty, and considering that an opportunity presented itself by which he might be useful to his country, at once offered himself a volunteer for this hazardous service. He passed in disguise to Long Island, and examined every part of the British army, and obtained the best possible information respecting their situation and future operations.

In his attempt to return, he was apprehended, carried before Sir William Howe, and the proof of his object was so clear, that he frankly acknowledged who he was, and what were his views. Sir William Howe at once gave an order to have him executed the next morning.

This order was accordingly executed in the most unfeeling manner, and by as great a savage as ever disgraced humanity. A clergyman, whose attendance he desired, was refused him; a Bible, for a few moments' devotion, was not procured, although he wished it. Letters which, on the morning of his execution, he wrote to his mother and other friends, were destroyed; and this very extraordinary reason given by the provost-martial, *"That the rebels should not know they had a man in their army who could die with so much firmness."*

Unknown to all around him, without a single friend to offer him the least consolation, thus fell as amiable and as worthy a young man as America could boast, with this as his dying observation, that *"he only lamented that he had but one life to lose for his country."*

Although the manner of this execution will ever be abhorred by every friend to humanity and religion, yet there cannot be a question but that the sentence was conformable to the rules of war, and the practice of nations in similar cases.

It is, however, but justice to the character of Captain Hale to observe, that his motives for engaging in this service were entirely different from those which generally influence others in similar circumstances. Neither expectation of promotion, nor pecuniary reward, induced him to this attempt. A sense of duty, a hope that he might in this way be useful to his country, and an opinion which he had adopted, that every kind of service necessary to the general good became honourable by being necessary, were the great motives which induced him to engage in an enterprise by which his connexions lost a most amiable friend, and his country one of its most promising supporters

The fate of this unfortunate young man excites the most interesting reflections. To see such a character, in the flower of youth, cheerfully treading in the most hazardous paths, influenced by the purest intentions, and only emulous to do good to his country, without the imputation of a crime, fall a victim to policy, must have been wounding to the feelings even of his enemies.

Should a comparison be drawn between Major Andre and Captain Hale, injustice would be done to the latter, should he not be placed on an equal ground with the former. While almost every historian of the American revolution has celebrated the virtues, and lamented the fate of Andre, Hale has remained unnoticed, and it is scarcely known such a character existed.

To the memory of Andre, his country has

erected the most magnificent monuments, and bestowed on his family the highest honours and most liberal rewards. To the memory of Hale, not a stone has been erected, nor an inscription to preserve his ashes from insult!

ISAAC HAYNE,

Colonel in the American Army.

"This gentleman had been a distinguished and very active officer in the American service, previous to the subjugation of Charleston When this event took place, he found himself called to a separation from his family, a dereliction of his property, and submission to the conqueror. In this situation he thought it his duty to become a voluntary prisoner, and take his parole. On surrendering himself, he offered to engage and stand bound on the principles of honour, to do nothing prejudicial to the British interest until he was exchanged; but his abilities and services were of such consideration to his country, that he was refused a parole, and told he must become a British subject, or submit to close confinement.

"His family was then in a distant part of the country, and in great distress by sickness, and from the ravages of the royalists in their neighbourhood. Thus he seemed impelled to acknowledge himself the subject of a government he had relinquished from the purest principles, or renounce his tenderest connexions, and leave them without a possibility of his assistance, and at a moment when he hourly expected to hear of the death of an affectionate wife, ill of the small-pox.

"In this state of anxiety, he subscribed a declaration of his allegiance to the king of Great Britain, with this express exception, that he should never be required to *take arms against his country*. Notwithstanding this, he was soon and repeatedly called upon to arm in support of a government he detested, or to submit to the severest punishment. Brigadier-General Patterson, commandant of the garrison, and the intendant of the British police, a Mr. Simpson, had both assured Colonel Hayne that no such thing would be required; and added, 'that when the royal army could not defend a country without the aid of its inhabitants, it would be time to quit it.'

"Colonel Hayne considered a requisition to act in British service, after assurances that this would never be required, as a breach of contract, and a release in the eye of conscience, from any obligation on his part. Accordingly he took the first opportunity of resuming his arms as an American, assumed the command of his own regiment; and all fond of their former commander, Colonel Hayne marched with a defensible body to the relief of his countrymen, then endeavouring to drive the British partizans, and keep them within the environs of Charleston. He very unfortunately, in a short time, fell into the hands of a strong British party, sent out for the recovery of a favourite officer, who had left the American cause, and become a devotee to the British government.

"As soon as Colonel Hayne was captured, he was closely imprisoned. This was on the twenty-sixth of July. He was notified the same day, that a court of officers would assemble the next day, to determine in what point of view he ought to be considered. On the twenty-ninth, he was informed that in consequence of a court of inquiry held the day before, Lord Rawdon and Lieutenant-Colonel Balfour had resolved upon his execution within two days.

"His astonishment at these summary and illegal proceedings can scarcely be conceived. He wrote Lord Rawdon that he had no intimation of any thing more than a court of inquiry, to determine whether he should be considered as an American or a British subject: if the first, he ought to be set at liberty on parole; if the last, he claimed a legal trial. He assured his lordship, that on a trial he had many things to urge in his defence; reasons that would be weighty in a court of equity; and concluded his letter with observing, 'If, sir, I am refused this favour, which I cannot conceive from your justice or humanity, I earnestly entreat that my execution may be deferred, that I may at least take a last farewell of my children, and prepare for the solemn change.'

"But his death predetermined, his enemies were deaf to the voice of compassion. The execution of his sentence was hastened, though he reputation and merits of this gentleman were such, that the whole city was zealous for his preservation. Not only the inhabitants in opposition to the British government, but even Lieutenant-Governor Bull, at the head of the royalists, interceded for his life. The principal ladies of Charleston endeavoured, by their compassionate interference, to arrest or influence the relentless hand of power. They drew up and presented to Lord Rawdon, a delicate and pathetic petition in his behalf. His near relations, and his children, who had just performed the funeral rites over the grave of a tender mother, appeared on their bended knees, to implore the life of their father. But in spite of the supplications of children and friends, strangers and foes, the flinty heart of Lord Rawdon remained untouched, amidst these scenes of sensibility and distress. No melioration of the sentence could be obtained; and this affectionate father took a final leave of his children in a manner that pierced the souls of the beholders. To the eldest of them, a youth of but thirteen years of age, he delivered a transcript of his case, directed him to convey it to Congress, and ordered him to see that his father's remains were deposited in the tomb of his ancestors.

"Pinioned like a criminal, this worthy citizen walked with composure through crowds of admiring spectators, with the dignity of the philosopher, and the intrepidity of the Christian. He suffered as a hero, and was hanged as a felon, amidst the tears of the multitude, and the curses of thousands, who execrated the perpetrators of this cruel deed."

CHARLES LEE,

MAJOR-GENERAL IN THE AMERICAN ARMY.

GENERAL LEE was an original genius, possessing the most brilliant talents, great military prowess, and extensive intelligence and knowledge of the world. He was born in Wales, his family springing from the same parent stock with the Earl of Leicester.

He may be properly called a child of Mars, for he was an officer when but eleven years old. His favourite study was the science of war, and his warmest wish was to become distinguished in it; but though possessed of a military spirit, he was ardent in the pursuit of general knowledge. He acquired a competent skill in Greek and Latin, while his fondness for travelling made him acquainted with the Italian, Spanish, German, and French languages.

In 1756, he came to America, captain of a company of grenadiers, and was present at the defeat of General Abercombie at Ticonderoga, where he received a severe wound. In 1762, he bore a colonel's commission, and served under Burgoyne in Portugal, where he greatly distinguished himself, and received the strongest recommendations for his gallantry; but his early attachment to the American colonies, evinced in his writings against the oppressive acts of parliament, lost him the favour of the ministry. Despairing of promotion, and despising a life of inactivity, he left his native soil, and entered into the service of his Polish majesty, as one of his aids, with the rank of major-general.

His rambling disposition led him to travel all over Europe, during the years of 1771, 1772, and part of 1773, and his warmth of temper drew him into several rencounters, among which was an affair of honour with an officer in Italy. The contest was begun with swords, when the general lost two of his fingers. Recourse was then had to pistols. His adversary was slain, and he was obliged to flee from the country, in order that he might avoid the unpleasant circumstances which might result from this unhappy circumstance.

General Lee appeared to be influenced by an innate principle of republicanism; an attachment to these principles was implanted in the constitution of his mind, and he espoused the cause of America as a champion of her emancipation from oppression.

Glowing with these sentiments, he embarked for this country, and arrived at New York on the 10th of November, 1773. On his arrival he became daily more enthusiastic in the cause of liberty, and travelled rapidly through the colonies, animating, both by conversation and his eloquent pen, to a determined and persevering resistance to British tyranny.

His enthusiasm in favour of the rights of the colonies was such, that, after the battle of Lexington, he accepted a major-general's commission in the American army; though his ambition had pointed out to him the post of commander-in-chief as the object of his wishes Previous to this, however, he resigned his commission in the British service, and relinquished his half-pay. This he did in a letter to the British secretary at war, in which he expressed his disapprobation of the oppressive measures of parliament, declaring them to be absolutely subversive of the rights and liberties of every individual subject, so destructive to the whole empire at large, and ultimately so ruinous to his majesty's own person, dignity, and family that he thought himself obliged in conscience, as a citizen, Englishman, and soldier of a free state, to exert his utmost to defeat them.

Immediately upon receiving his appointment, he accompanied General Washington to the camp at Cambridge, where he arrived July 2d, 1775, and was received with every mark of respect.

As soon as it was discovered at Cambridge that the British General Clinton had left Boston, General Lee was ordered to set forward, to observe his manœuvres, and prepare to meet him in any part of the continent he might visit. No man was better qualified, at this early stage of the war, to penetrate the designs of the enemy, than Lee. Nursed in the camp, and well versed in European tactics, the soldiers believed him, of all other officers, the best abl to face in the field an experienced British veteran, and lead them on to victory.

New York was supposed to be the object of the enemy, and hither he hastened with all possible expedition. Immediately on his arrival, Lee took the most active and prompt measures to put it in a state of defence. He disarmed all suspected persons within the reach of his command, and proceeded with such rigour against the tories, as to give alarm at his assumption of military powers. From the tories he exacted a strong oath, and his bold measures carried terror wherever he appeared.

"Not long after he was appointed to the command of the southern department, and in his travels through the country, he received every testimony of high respect from the people. General Sir Henry Clinton, and Sir Peter Parker, with a powerful fleet and army, attempted the reduction of Charleston while he was in command. The fleet anchored within half musket-shot of the fort on Sullivan's Island, where Col. Moultrie, one of the bravest and most intrepid of men, commanded. A tremendous engagement ensued on the 28th of June, 1776, which lasted twelve hours without intermission. The whole British force was completely repulsed, after suffering an irreparable loss.

"General Lee and Colonel Moultrie received the thanks of Congress for their signal bravery and gallantry.

"Our hero had now reached the pinnacle of his military glory; the eclat of his name alone appeared to enchant and animate the most desponding heart. But here we pause to conemplate the humiliating reverse of human events. He returned to the main army in October; and in marching at the head of a large detachment through the Jerseys, having, from a desire of retaining a separate command, delayed his march several days, in disobedience of express orders from the commander-in-chief, he was guilty of most culpable negligence in regard to his personal security. He took up his quarters two or three miles from the main body, and lay for the night, December 13th, 1776, in a careless, exposed situation. Information of this being communicated to Colonel Harcourt, who commanded the British light-horse, he proceeded immediately to the house, fired into it, and obliged the general to surrender himself a prisoner. They mounted him on a horse in haste, without his cloak or hat, and conveyed him in triumph to New York."

Lee was treated, while a prisoner, with great severity by the enemy, who affected to consider him as a state prisoner and deserter from the service of his Britannic majesty, and denied the privileges of an American officer. General Washington promptly retaliated the treatment received by Lee upon the British officers in his possession. This state of things existed until the capture of Burgoyne, when a complete change of treatment was observed towards Lee; and he was shortly afterward exchanged.

The first military act of General Lee after his exchange, closed his career in the American army. Previous to the battle of Monmouth, his character in general was respectable. From the beginning of the contest, his unremitted zeal in the cause of America excited and directed the military spirit of the whole continent; and his conversation inculcated the principles of liberty among all ranks of the people.

His important services excited the warm gratitude of many of the friends of America. Hence it is said that a strong party was formed in Congress, and by some discontented officers in the army, to raise Lee to the first command: and it has been suggested by many, that General Lee's conduct at the battle of Monmouth was intended to effect this plan: for could the odium of the defeat have been at this time thrown on General Washington, there is great reason to suppose that he would have been deprived of his command.

It is now to be seen how General Lee termi

nated his military career. In the battle of Monmouth, on the 28th of June, 1778, he commanded the van of the American troops, with orders from the commander-in-chief to attack the retreating enemy. Instead of obeying this order, he conducted in an unworthy manner, and greatly disconcerted the arrangements of the day. Washington, advancing to the field of battle, met him in his disorderly retreat, and accosted him with strong expressions of disapprobation. Lee, incapable of brooking even an implied indignity, and unable to restrain the warmth of his resentment, used improper language in return, and some iritation was excited on both sides. The following letters immediately after passed between Lee and the commander-in-chief:

Camp, English-Town, 1st July, 1778.
SIR—From the knowledge that I have of your excellency's character, I must conclude that nothing but the misinformation of some very stupid, or misrepresentation of some very wicked person, could have occasioned your making use of such very singular expressions as you did, on my coming up to the ground where you had taken post: they implied that

I was guilty either of disobedience of orders, want of conduct, or want of courage. Your excellency will, therefore, infinitely oblige me by letting me know on which of these three articles you ground your charge, that I may prepare for my justification; which I have the happiness to be confident I can do to the army, to the Congress, to America, and to the world in general. Your excellency must give me leave to observe, that neither yourself, nor those about your person, could, from your situation, be in the least judges of the merits or demerits of our manœuvres; and, to speak with a becoming pride, I can assert that to these manœuvres the success of the day was entirely owing. I can boldly say, that had we remained on the first ground—or had we advanced—or had the retreat been conducted in a manner different from what it was, this whole army, and the interests of America, would have risked being sacrificed. I ever had, and I hope ever shall have, the greatest respect and veneration for General Washington; I think him endowed with many great and good qualities; but in this instance I must pronounce, that he has been guilty of an act of cruel injustice towards a man who had certainly some pretensions to the regard of every servant of his country; and I think, sir, I have a right to demand some reparation for the injury committed; and unless I can obtain it, I must, in justice to myself, when the campaign is closed, which I believe will close the war, retire from a service, at the head of which is placed a man capable of offering such injuries;—but at the same time, in justice to you, I must repeat that I, from my soul, believe that it was not a motion of your own breast, but instigated by some of those dirty earwigs, who will for ever insinuate themselves near persons in high office; for I am really assured that, when General Washington acts from himself, no man in his army will have reason to complain of injustice and indecorum.

I am, sir, and I hope ever shall have reason to continue, Yours, &c.

CHARLES LEE.

His excellency General Washington.

Head-quarters, English-Town, June 28, 1778

Sir—I received your letter, dated through mistake the 1st of July, expressed, as I conceive, in terms highly improper. I am not conscious of having made use of any singular expressions at the time of my meeting you, as you intimate. What I recollect to have said was dictated by duty, and warranted by the occasion. As soon as circumstances will admit, you shall have an opportunity, either of justifying yourself to the army, to Congress, to America, and to the world in general, or of convincing them that you are guilty of a breach of orders, and of misbehaviour before the enemy on the 28th instant, in not attacking them as you had been directed, and in making an unnecessary, disorderly, and shameful retreat.

I am, sir, your most obedient servant,
G. WASHINGTON.

A court-martial, of which Lord Stirling was president, was ordered for his trial, and after a masterly defence by General Lee, found him guilty of all the charges, and sentenced him to be suspended from any command in the army for the term of twelve months. This sentence was shortly afterward confirmed by Congress.

When promulgated, it was like a mortal wound to the lofty, aspiring spirit of General Lee; pointing to his dog, he exclaimed—"Oh that I was that animal, that I might not call man my brother." He became outrageous, and from that moment he was more open and virulent in his attack on the character of the commander-in-chief, and did not cease in his unwearied endeavours, both in his conversation and writings, to lessen his reputation in the estimation of the army and the public. He was an active abettor of General Conway in his calumny and abuse of General Washington, and they were believed to be in concert in their vile attempts to supersede his excellency in the supreme command. With the hope of effecting his nefarious purpose, he published a pamphlet replete with scurrilous imputations unfavourable to the military talents of the commander-in-chief, but this, with his other malignant allegations, was consigned to contempt.

At length Colonel Laurens, one of General Washington's aids, unable longer to suffer this gross abuse of his illustrious friend, demanded of Lee that satisfaction which custom has sanctioned as honourable. A rencounter accordingly ensued, and Lee received a wound in his side.

Lee now finding himself abandoned by his friends, degraded in the eye of the public, and despised by the wise and virtuous, retired to his sequestered plantation in Virginia. In this spot, secluded from all society, he lived in a sort of hovel, without glass windows or plastering, or even a decent article of house furniture; here he amused himself with his books and dogs. On January 10th, 1780, Congress resolved that Major-General Lee be informed that they have no further occasion for his services in the army of the United States. In the autumn of 1782, wearied with his forlorn situation and broken spirit, he resorted to Philadelphia, and took lodgings in an ordinary tavern. He was soon seized with a disease of the lungs, and after a few days' confinement, he terminated his mortal course, a martyr to chagrin and disappointment, October 2d, 1782. The last words which he was heard to utter were, "stand by me, my brave grenadiers."

General Lee was rather above the middle size, " plain in his person even to ugliness, and careless in his manners even to a degree of rudeness: his nose was so remarkably aquiline, that it appeared as a real deformity. His voice was rough, his garb ordinary, his deportment morose. He was ambitious of fame, without the dignity to support it. In private life he sunk into the vulgarity of the clown." His remarkable partiality for dogs was such, that a number of these animals constantly followed in his train, and the ladies complained that he allowed his *canine adherents* to follow him into the parlour, and not unfrequently a favourite one might be seen on a chair next his elbow at table.

In the year 1776, when our army lay at White-Plains, Lee resided near the road which General Washington frequently passed, and he one day with his aids called and took dinner. After they had departed, Lee said to his aids, "You must look me out other quarters, or I shall have Washington and his puppies calling till they eat me up." The next day he ordered his servants to write with chalk on the door, "No victuals cooked here to-day." The company seeing the hint on the door, passed, with a smile at the oddity of the man. "The character of this person," says one who knew him well, "is full of absurdities and qualities of a most extraordinary nature."

While in Philadelphia, shortly before his death, the following ludicrous circumstance took place, which created no small diversion.

The late Judge Brackenridge, whose poignancy of satire and eccentricity of character were nearly a match for that of the general, had dipped his pen in some gall, which greatly irritated Lee's feelings, insomuch that he challenged him to single combat, which Brackenridge declined in a very eccentric reply. Lee having furnished himself with a horsewhip, determined to chastise him ignominiously on the very first opportunity. Observing Brackenridge going down Market street a few days after, he gave him chase, and Brackenridge took refuge in a public house, and barricadoed the door of the room he entered. A number of persons collected to see the result. Lee damned him, and invited him to come out and fight him like a man. Brackenridge replied, that he did not like to be shot at, and made some other curious observations, which only increased Lee's irritation, and the mirth of the spectators. Lee, with the most bitter imprecation, ordered him to come out, when he said he would horsewhip him. Brackenridge replied, that he had no occasion for a discipline of that kind. The amusing scene lasted some time, until at length Lee, finding that he could accomplish no other object than calling forth Brackenridge's wit for the amusement of the bystanders, retired.

General Lee was master of a most genteel

address, but was rude in his manners, and excessively negligent in his appearance and behaviour. His appetite was so whimsical, that he was every where a most troublesome guest. Two or three dogs usually followed him wherever he went. As an officer, he was brave and able, and did much towards disciplining the American army. With vigorous powers of mind and a brilliant fancy, he was a correct and elegant classical scholar, and he both wrote and spoke his native language with propriety, force, and beauty. His temper was severe; the history of his life is little else than the history of disputes, quarrels, and duels, in every part of the world. He was vindictive, avaricious, immoral, impious, and profane. His principles, as would be expected from his character, were most abandoned, and he ridiculed every tenet of religion. Two virtues he possessed to an eminent degree, sincerity and veracity. It was notorious that General Lee was a man of unbounded personal ambition; and, conscious of his European education, and pre-eminent military talents and prowess, he effected a superiority over General Washington, and constantly aimed at the supreme command, little scrupu lous as to the means employed to accomplish his own advancement.

The following is an extract from General Lee's will.

"I desire most earnestly that I may not be buried in any church or church-yard, or within a mile of any Presbyterian or Anabaptist meeting house; for since I have resided in this country, I have kept so much bad company while living, that I do not choose to continue it while dead."

JOHN SULLIVAN,

MAJOR-GENERAL IN THE AMERICAN ARMY.

General Sullivan was a native of New Hampshire, where he resided before the revolution, and attained to a high degree of eminence in the profession of the law. He was a member of the first Congress, in 1774; but on the commencement of hostilities, preferring a military commission, he relinquished the fairest prospects of fortune and fame, and appeared among the most ardent patriots and intrepid warriors.

"In 1775, he was appointed a brigadier general, and immediately joined the army at Cambridge, and soon after obtained the command on Winter Hill. The next year he was ordered to Canada, and, on the death of General Thomas, the command of the army devolved on him. The situation of our army in that quarter was inexpressibly distressing; destitute of clothing, dispirited by defeat and constant fatigue, and a large proportion of the troops sick with the small-pox. By his great exertions and judicious management, he meliorated the condition of the army, and obtained general applause. On his retiring from that command July 12th, 1776, the field-officers thus addressed him: 'It is to you, sir, the public are indebted for the preservation of their property in Canada. It is to you we owe our safety thus far. Your humanity will call forth the silent tear and the grateful ejaculation of the sick. Your universal impartiality will force the applause of the wearied soldier.'

"In August, 1776, he was promoted to the rank of major-general, and soon after was, with Major-General Lord Stirling, captured by the British in the battle on Long Island. General Sullivan being paroled, was sent by General Howe with a message to Congress, after which he returned to New York. In September he was exchanged for Major General Prescott. We next find him in command of the right division of our troops, in the famous battle at Trenton, and he acquitted himself honourably on that ever memorable day.

"In August, 1777, without the authority of Congress, or the commander-in-chief, he planned and executed an expedition against the enemy on Staten Island. Though the enterprise was conducted with prudence and success, in part, it was said by some to have been less brilliant than might have been expected under his favourable circumstances; and as that act was deemed a bold assumption of responsibility, and reports to his prejudice being in circulation, a court of inquiry was ordered to investigate his conduct. The result was an honourable acquittal; and Congress resolved, that the result, so honourable to General Sullivan, is highly pleasing to Congress, and that the opinion of the court be published, in justification of that injured officer.

"In the battles of Brandywine and Germantown, in the autumn of 1777, General Sullivan commanded a division, and in the latter conflict his two aids were killed, and his own conduct was so conspicuously brave, that General Washington, in his letter to Congress, concludes with encomiums on the gallantry of General Sullivan, and the whole right wing of the army, who acted immediately under the eye of his excel.ency.

"In August, 1778, General Sullivan, was sole commander of an expedition to the Island of Newport, in co-operation with the French fleet under the Count D'Estaing. The Marquis de la Fayette and General Greene volunteered their services on the occasion. The object of the expedition was defeated, in consequence of the French fleet being driven off by a violent storm. By this unfortunate event, the enemy were encouraged to engage our army in battle, in which they suffered a repulse, and General Sullivan finally effected a safe retreat to the main. This retreat, so ably executed, without confusion or the loss of baggage or stores, increased the military reputation of General Sullivan, and redounds to his honour as a skilful commander.

"The bloody tragedy acted at Wyoming, in 1778, had determined the commander-in-chief, in 1779, to employ a large detachment from the continental army to penetrate into the heart of the Indian country, to chastise the hostile tribes and their white associates and adherents, for their cruel aggressions on the defenceless inhabitants. The command of this expedition was committed to Major-General Sullivan, with express orders to destroy their settlements, to ruin their crops, and make such thorough devastations as to render the country entirely uninhabitable for the present, and thus to compel the savages to remove to a greater distance from our frontiers.

"General Sullivan had under his command several brigadiers, and a well chosen army, to which were attached a number of friendly Indian warriors. With this force he penetrated about ninety miles, through a horrid swampy wilderness and barren mountainous deserts, to Wyoming, on the Susquehanna river, thence by water to Tioga, and possessed himself of numerous towns and villages of the savages.

"During this hazardous expedition General Sullivan and his army encountered the most complicated obstacles, requiring the greatest fortitude and perseverance to surmount. He explored an extensive tract of country, and strictly executed the severe, but necessary orders he had received. A considerable number of Indians were slain, some were captured, their habitations were burnt, and their plantations of corn and vegetables laid waste in the most effectual manner. 'Eighteen villages, a number of detached buildings, one hundred and sixty thousand bushels of corn, and those fruits and vegetables which conduce to the comfort and subsistence of man, were utterly destroyed. Five weeks were unremittingly employed in this work of devastation.'

"On his return from the expedition, he and his army received the approbation of Congress. It is remarked on this expedition, by the translator of M. Chastelleux's travels, an Englishman, then resident in the United States, that the instructions given by General Sullivan to his officers, the order of march he prescribed to his troops, and the discipline he had the ability to maintain, would have done honour to the most experienced ancient or modern generals.

"At the close of the campaign of 1779, General Sullivan, in consequence of impaired health, resigned his commission in the army. Congress, in accepting his resignation, passed a resolve, thanking him for his past services. His military talents and bold spirit of enterprise were universally acknowledged. He was fond of display, and his personal appearance and dignified deportment commanded respect. After his resignation, he resumed his professional pursuits at the bar, and was much distinguished as a statesman, politician, and patriot. He acquired very considerable proficiency in general literature, and an exten sive knowledge of men and the world. He received from Harvard University a degree of master of arts, and from the University of Dartmouth a degree of doctor of laws. He was one of the convention who formed the state constitution for New Hampshire, was chosen into the first council, and was afterwards elected chief magistrate in that state, and held the office for three years. In September, 1789, he was appointed judge of the district court for the district of New Hampshire, and continued in the office till his death, in 1795."

JOSEPH WARREN,

Major-General in the American Army.

"Joseph Warren was born in Roxbury, near Boston, in the year 1741. His father was a respectable farmer in that place, who had held several municipal offices, to the acceptance of his fellow citizens. Joseph, with several of his brothers, was instructed in the elementary branches of knowledge, at the public grammar-school of the town, which was distinguished for its successive instructers of superior attainments. In 1755, he entered college, where he sustained the character of a youth of talents, fine manners, and of a generous independent deportment, united to great personal courage and perseverance. An anecdote will illustrate his fearlessness and determination at that age, when character can hardly be said to be formed. Several students of Warren's class shut themselves in a room to arrange some college affairs, in a way which they knew was contrary to his wishes, and barred the door so effectually, that he could not without great violence force it: but he did

not give over the attempt of getting among them; for perceiving that the window of the room in which they were assembled was open, and near a spout which extended from the roof of the building to the ground, he went to the top of the house, slid down to the eaves, seized the spout, and when he had descended as far as the window, threw himself into the chamber among them. At that instant the spout, which was decayed and weak, gave way and fell to the ground. He looked at it without emotion, said that it had served his purpose, and began to take his part in the business. A spectator of this feat and narrow escape, related this fact to me in the college-yard, nearly half a century afterward; and the impression it made on his mind was so strong, that he seemed to feel the same emotion as though it had happened but an hour before.

"On leaving college, in 1759, Warren turned his attention to the study of medicine, under the direction of Doctor Lloyd, an eminent physician of that day, whose valuable life has been protracted almost to the present time. Warren was distinguished very soon after he commenced practice: for when, in

1764, the small-pox spread in Boston, he was among the most successful in his method of treating that disease, which was then considered the most dreadful scourge of the human race; and the violence of which had baffled the efforts of the learned faculty of medicine from the time of its first appearance. From this moment he stood high among his brethren, and was the favourite of the people; and what he gained in their good-will he never lost. His personal appearance, his address, his courtesy, and his humanity, won the way to the hearts of all; and his knowledge and superiority of talents secured the conquest. A bright and lasting fame in his profession, with the attendant consequences, wealth and influence, were within his reach, and near at hand: but the calls of a distracted country were paramount to every consideration of his own interests, and he entered the vortex of politics, never to return to the peaceful course of professional labour.

"The change in public opinion had been gradually preparing the minds of most men for a revolution. This was not openly avow-·d: amelioration of treatment for the present, and assurances of kindness in future, were all

that the colonies asked from Great Britain— but
these they did not receive. The mother country
mistook the spirit of her children, and used
threats when kindness would have been the
best policy. When Britain declared her right
to direct, govern, and tax us in any form, and
at all times, the colonies reasoned, remonstrated, and entreated for a while; and when
these means did not answer, they defied and
resisted. The political writers of the province
had been active and busy, but they were generally screened by fictitious names, or sent their
productions anonymously into the world; but
the time had arrived, when speakers of nerve
and boldness were wanted to raise their voices
against oppression in every shape. Warren
possessed first rate qualities for an orator, and
had early declared in the strongest terms his
political sentiments, which were somewhat in
advance of public opinion; for he held as
tyranny all taxation which could be imposed
by the British parliament upon the colonies.
In times of danger, the people are sagacious,
and cling to those who best can serve them;
and every eye was on him in every emergency;
for he had not only the firmness and decision
they wished for in a leader, but was prudent

and wary in all his plans. His first object was to enlighten the people; and then he felt sure of engaging their feelings in the general cause. He knew, when once they began, it would be impossible to tread back—independence only would satisfy the country. With an intention of directing public sentiment, without appearing to be too active, he met frequently with a considerable number of substantial mechanics, and others in the middling classes of society, who were busy in politics. This crisis required such a man as they found him to be; one who could discern the signs of the times, and mould the ductile materials to his will, and at the same time seem only to follow in the path of others. His letter to Barnard, which attracted the notice of government, had been written several years before, in 1768; but in some form or other he was constantly enlightening the people by his pen: but it is now difficult, and of no great importance, to trace him in the papers of that period. The public was not then always right in designating the authors of political essays. In the different situations in which he was called to act, he assumed as many characters as fable has ever given to the tutelar god of his profession, and like him, in every one of them, he retained the wisdom to guide and the power to charm. At one time he might be found restraining the impetuosity, and bridling the fury of those hot-headed politicians who felt more than they reasoned, and dared to do more than became men. Such was his versatility, that he turned from these lectures of caution and prudence, to asserting and defending the most bold and undisguised principles of liberty, and defying, in their very teeth, the agents of the crown. Twice he was elected to deliver the oration on the 5th of March, in commemoration of the *massacre;* and his orations are among the most distinguished produced by that splendid list of speakers who addressed their fellow citizens on this subject, so interesting to them all. In these productions generally, the immediate causes of this event were overlooked, and the remote ones alone were discussed. Here they were on safe ground; for tyranny, in its incipient stages, has no excuses from opposition; but in its march, it generally finds some plausible arguments for its proceedings, drawn from the very resistance it naturally produces. These occasions gave the orators a fine field for remark, and a fair opportunity for effect. The great orators of antiquity, in their speeches, attempted only to rouse the people to retain what they possessed. Invective, entreaty, and pride, had their effect in assisting those mighty masters to influence the people, They were ashamed to lose what their fathers left them, won by their blood, and so long preserved by their wisdom, their virtues, and their courage. Our statesmen had a harder task to perform; for they were compelled to call on the people to gain what they had never enjoyed—an independent rank and standing among the nations of the world.

"His next oration was delivered March 6th, 1775. It was at his own solicitation that he was appointed to this duty a second time. The fact is illustrative of his character, and worthy of remembrance. Some British officers of the army then in Boston, had publicly declared that it should be at the price of the life of any man to speak of the event of March 5th, 1770, on that anniversary. Warren's soul took fire at such a threat, so openly made, and he wished for the honour of braving it. This was readily granted: for at such a time a man would probably find but few rivals. Many who would spurn the thought of personal fear might be apprehensive that they would be so far disconcerted as to forget their discourse. It is easier to fight bravely, than to think clearly or correctly in danger. Passion sometimes nerves the arm to fight, but disturbs the regular current of thought. The day came, and the weather was remarkably fine. The Old South Meeting House was crowded at an early hour. The British officers occupied the aisles, the flight of steps to the pulpit, and several of them were within it. It was not precisely known whether this was accident or design. The orator, with the assistance of his friends, made his entrance at the pulpit window by a ladder. The officers seeing his coolness and intrepedity, made way for him to advance and address the audience. An awful stillness preceded his exordium. Each man felt the palpitations of his own heart, and saw the pale but determined face of his neighbour. The speaker began his oration in a firm tone of voice, and proceeded with great energy and pathos. Warren and his friends were prepared to chastise contumely, prevent disgrace, and avenge an attempt at assassination.

"The scene was sublime; a patriot, in whom the flush of youth and the grace and dignity of manhood were combined, stood armed in the sanctuary of God, to animate and encourage the sons of liberty, and to hurl defiance at their oppressors. The orator commenced with the early history of the country, described the tenure by which we held our liberties and property—the affection we had constantly shown the parent country, and boldly told them how, and by whom these blessings of life had been violated. There was in this appeal to Britain—in this description of suffering, agony, and horror, a calm and high-souled defiance which must have chilled the blood of every sensible foe. Such another hour has seldom happened in the history of man, and is not surpassed in the records of nations. The thunders of Demosthenes rolled at a distance from Philip and his host—and Tully poured the fiercest torrent of his invective when Cataline was at a distance, and his dagger no longer to be feared: but Warren's speech was made to proud oppressors, resting on their arms, whose errand it was to overawe, and whose business it was to fight.

"If the deed of Brutus deserved to be commemorated by history, poetry, painting, and sculpture, should not this instance of patriotism and bravery be held in lasting remembrance? If he

> 'That struck the foremost man of all this world.'

was hailed as the first of freeman, what honours are not due to him, who undismayed bearded the British lion, to show the world what his countrymen dared to do in the cause of liberty? If the statue of Brutus was placed among those of the gods who were the preservers of Roman freedom, should not that of Warren fill a lofty niche in the temple reared to perpetuate the remembrance of our birth as a nation?

"If independence was not at first openly avowed by our leading men at that time, the hope of attaining it was fondly cherished, and the exertions of the patriots pointed to this end. The wise knew that the storm which the political Prosperos were raising, would pass away in blood. With these impressions on his mind, Warren for several years was preparing himself by study and observation, to take a conspicuous rank in the military arrangements which he knew must ensue.

"On the 18th of April, 1775, by his agents in Boston, he discovered the design of the

British commander to sieze or destroy our few stores at Concord. He instantly despatched several confidential messengers to Lexington. The late venerable patriot, Paul Revere, was one of them. This gentleman has given a very interesting account of the difficulties he encountered in the discharge of this duty. The alarm was given, and the militia, burning with resentment, were, at day-break on the 19th, on the road to repel insult and aggression. The drama was opened about sunrise, within a few yards of the house of God, in Lexington. Warren hastened to the field of action, in the full ardour of his soul, and shared the dangers of the day. While pressing on the enemy, a musket-ball took off a lock of his hair close to his ear. The lock was rolled and pinned, after the fashion of that day, and considerable force must have been necessary to have cut it away. The people were delighted with his cool, collected bravery, and already considered him as a leader, whose gallantry they were to admire, and in whose talents they were to confide. On the 14th of June, 1775, the Provincial Congress of Massachusetts made him a major-general of their forces; but previous to the date of his commission, he had been unceasing in his exertions to maintain order and enforce discipline among the troops, which had hastily assembled at Cambridge, after the battle of Lexington. He mingled in the ranks, and by every method and argument strove to inspire them with confidence, and succeeded in a most wonderful manner in imparting to them a portion of the flame which glowed in his own breast. At such a crisis genius receives its birth-right—the homage of inferior minds, who, for self-preservation, are willing to be directed. Previous to receiving the appointment of major-general, he had been requested to take the office of physician-general to the army, but he chose to be where wounds were to be made, rather than where they were to be healed. Yet he lent his aid and advice to the medical department of the army, and was of great service to them in their organization and arrangements.

"He was at this time president of the Provincial Congress, having been elected, the preceding year, a member from the town of Boston. In this body he discovered his extraordinary powers of mind, and his peculiar fitness for responsible offices at such a juncture.

Cautious in proposing measures, he was assiduous in pursuing what he thought, after mature deliberation, to be right, and never counted the probable cost of a measure, when he had decided that it was necessary to be taken. When this Congress, which was sitting at Watertown, adjourned for the day, he mounted his horse and hastened to the camp. Every day 'he bought golden opinions of all sorts of men;' and when the troops were called to act on Breed's Hill, he had so often been among them, that his person was known to most of the soldiers.

"Several respectable historians have fallen into some errors in describing the battle in which he fell, by giving the command of the troops on that day to Warren, when he was only a volunteer in the fight. He did not arrive on the battle-ground until the enemy had commenced their movements for the attack. As soon as he made his appearance on the field, the veteran commander of the day, Colonel Prescott, desired to act under his directions; but Warren declined taking any other part than that of a volunteer, and added, that he came to learn the art of war from an experienced soldier, whose orders he should be happy to obey. In the battle he was armed with a musket, and stood in the ranks, now and then changing his place, to encourage his fellow-soldiers by words and by example. He undoubtedly, from the state of hostilities, expected soon to act in his high military capacity, and it was indispensable, according to his views, that he should share the dangers of the field as a common soldier with his fellow-citizens, that his reputation for bravery might be put beyond the possibility of suspicion. The wisdom of such a course would never have been doubted, if he had returned in safety from the fight. In such a struggle for independence, the ordinary rules of prudence and caution could not govern those who were building up their names for future usefulness by present exertion. Some maxims drawn from the republican writers of antiquity, were worn as their mottos. Some precepts descriptive of the charms of liberty, were ever on their tongues; and some classical model of Greek or Roman patriotism was constantly in their minds. Instances of great men mixing in the rank of common soldiers, were to be found in ancient times, when men fought for their altars and their homes. The cases were parallel, and the examples were imposing. When the battle was decided, and our people fled, Warren was one of the last who left the breastwork, and was slain within a few yards of it, as he was slowly retiring. He probably felt mortified at the event of the day; but had he known how dearly the victory was purchased, and how little honour was gained by those who won it, his heart would have been at rest. Like the band of Leonidas, the vanquished have received, by the judgment of nations, from which there is no appeal, the imperishable laurels of victors. His death brought a sickness to the heart of the community, and the people mourned his fall, not with the convulsive agony of a betrothed virgin over the bleeding corpse of her lover—but with the pride of the Spartan mother, who, in the intensity of her grief, smiled to see that the wounds whence life had flown, were on the breast of her son—and was satisfied that he had died in defence of his country. The worth of the victim, and the horror of the sacrifice, gave a higher value to our liberties, and produced a more fixed determination to preserve them.

"The battle of Bunker's Hill has often been

described, and of late its minutest details given to the public; but never was the military, moral, and political character of that great event more forcibly drawn, than in the following extract from the North American Review, for July, 1818:

'The incidents and the result of the battle itself, were most important, and indeed most wonderful. As a mere battle, few surpass it in whatever engages and interests the attention. It was fought on a conspicuous eminence, in the immediate neighbourhood of a populous city; and consequently in the view of thousands of spectators. The attacking army moved over a sheet of water to the assault. The operations and movements were of course all visible and all distinct. Those who looked on from the houses and heights of Boston had a fuller view of every important operation and event, than can ordinarily be had of any battle or that can possibly be had of such as are fought on a more extended ground, or by detachments of troops acting in different places, and at different times, and in some measure independently of each other. When the British columns were advancing to the attack, the flames of Charlestown, (fired, as is generally supposed, by a shell,) began to ascend. The spectators, far outnumbering both armies, thronged and crowded on every height and every point which afforded a view of the scene, themselves constituting a very important part of it.

'The troops of the two armies seemed like so many combatants in an amphitheatre. The manner in which they should acquit themselves was to be judged of, not as in other cases of military engagements, by reports and future history, but by a vast and anxious assembly already on the spot, and waiting with unspeakable concern and emotion the progress of the day.

'In other battles, the *recollection* of wives and children has been used as an excitement to animate the warrior's breast, and nerve his arm. Here was not a mere recollection, but an actual *presence* of them and other dear connexions, hanging on the skirts of the battle, anxious and agitated, feeling almost as if wounded themselves by every blow of the enemy, and putting forth, as it were, their own strength, and all the energy of their own throbbing bosoms, into every gallant effort of their warring friends.

'But there was a more comprehensive, and vastly more important view of that day's contest, than has been mentioned; a view, indeed, which ordinary eyes, bent intently on what was immediately before them, did not embrace, but which was perceived in its full extent and expansion by minds of a higher order. Those men who were at the head of the colonial councils, who had been engaged for years in the previous stages of the quarrel with England, and who had been accustomed to look forward to the future, were well apprised of the magnitude of the events likely to hang on the business of that day. They saw in it not only a battle, but the beginning of a civil war, of unmeasured extent and uncertain issue. All America, and all England, were likely to be deeply concerned in the consequences. The individuals themselves, who knew full well what agency they had had in bringing affairs to this crisis, had need of all their courage: not that disregard of personal safety, in which the vulgar suppose true courage to consist, but that high and fixed moral sentiment, that steady and decided purpose, which enables men to pursue a distant end with a full view of the difficulties and dangers before them, and with a conviction that, before they arrive at the proposed end, should they ever reach it, they must pass through evil report as well as good report, and be liable to obloquy as well as to defeat.

'Spirits that fear nothing else, fear disgrace; and this danger is necessarily encountered by those who engage in civil war. Unsuccessful resistance is not only ruin to its authors, but is esteemed, and necessarily so, by the laws of all countries, treasonable. This is the case, at least till resistance becomes so general and formidable as to assume the form of regular war. But who can tell, when resistance commences, whether it will attain even to that degree of success? Some of those persons who signed the Declaration of Independence, in 1777, described themselves as signing it, 'as with halters about their necks.' If there were grounds for this remark in 1776, when the cause had become so much more general, how much greater was the hazard when the battle of Bunker-Hill was fought!

'These considerations constituted, to enlarged and liberal minds, the moral sublimity of the occasion; while, to the outward senses, the movement of armies, the roar of artillery, the brilliancy of the reflection of a summer's sun from the burnished armour of the British columns, and the flames of a burning town, made up a scene of extraordinary grandeur.'

"This eminence has become sacred ground. It contains in its bosom the ashes of the brave who died fighting to defend their altars and their homes. Strangers from all countries visit this spot, for it is associated in their memories with Marathon and Platæa, and all the mighty struggles of determined freemen. Our citizens love to wander over this field—they agreed to awake recollections, and the youthful to excite heroic emotions. The battle-ground is now all plainly to be seen—the spirit of modern improvement, which would stop the streams of Helicon to turn a mill, and caused to be felled the trees of Paradise to make a rafter, has yet spared this hallowed height.

"If 'the days of chivalry be gone for ever,' and the high and enthusiastic feelings of generosity and magnanimity be not so widely diffused as in more heroic ages, yet it cannot be denied but that there have been, and still are, individuals whose bosoms are warmed with a spirit as glowing and ethereal as ever swelled the heart of 'mailed knight,' who, in the ecstacies of love, religion, and martial glory, joined the war-cry on the plains of Palestine, or proved his steel on the infidel foe. The history of every revolution is interspersed with brilliant episodes of individual prowess. The pages of our own history, when fully written out, will sparkle profusely with these gems of romantic valour.

"The calmness and indifference of the veteran ' in clouds of dust, and seas of blood,' can only be acquired by long acquaintance with the trade of death; but the heights of Charlestown will bear eternal testimony how suddenly, in the cause of freedom, the peaceful citizen can become the invincible warrior —stung by oppression, he springs forward from his tranquil pursuits, undaunted by opposition, and undismayed by danger, to fight even to death for the defence of his rights. Parents, wives, children, and country, all the hallowed properties of existence, are to him the talisman that takes fear from his heart, and nerves his arm to victory.

"In the requiem over those who have fallen in the cause of their country, which

'Time with his own eternal lips shall sing,'

the praises of WARREN shall be distinctly heard. The blood of those patriots who have fallen in the defence of republics, has often 'cried from the ground' against the ingratitude of the country for which it was shed. No monument was reared to their fame; no record of their virtues written; no fostering hand extended to their offspring—but they and their deeds were neglected and forgotten. Toward Warren there was no ingratitude—our country is free from this stain. Congress were the guardians of his honour, and remembered that his children were unprotected orphans. Within a year after his death Congress passed the following resolutions:

"That a monument be erected to the memory of General Warren, in the town of Boston, with the following inscription:

IN HONOUR OF
JOSEPH WARREN,
Major-General, of Massachusetts-Bay.
He devoted his Life to the
Liberties of his Country,
and, in bravely defending them,
fell an early Victim in the

BATTLE OF BUNKER-HILL,
June 17, 1775.
The Congress of the United States,
as an acknowledgment of his
Services and distinguished
Merit, have erected this
Monument to his
memory.

"It was resolved, likewise, 'that the eldest son of General Warren should be educated, from that time, at the expense of the United States.' On the 1st of July, 1780, Congress, recognising these former resolutions, further resolved, 'That it should be recommended to the executive of Massachusetts-Bay to make provision for the maintenance and education of his three younger children. And that Congress would defray the expense to the amount of the half-pay of a major-general, to commence at the time of his death, and continue till the youngest of the children should be of age.' The part of the resolutions relating to the education of the children, was carried into effect accordingly. The monument is not yet erected, but it is not too late."

JOHN LAURENS,

Colonel in the American Army,

"Son of Henry Laurens, was born in Charleston, in 1755. In youth he discovered that energy of character which distinguished him through life. When a lad, though labouring under a fever, on the cry of fire, he leaped from his bed, hastened to the scene of danger, and was in a few minutes on the top of the exposed houses, risking his life to arrest the progress of the flames. This is the more worthy of notice, for precisely in the same way, and under a similar, but higher impulse of ardent patriotism, he lost his life in the year 1782.

"At the age of sixteen he was taken to Europe by his father, and there put under the best means of instruction in Geneva, and afterward in London.

"He was entered a student of law at the temple in 1774, and was daily improving in legal knowledge till the disputes between Great Britain and her colonies arrested his attention. He soon found that the claims of the mother country struck at the root of liberty in the colonies, and that she perseveringly resolved to enforce these claims at every hazard. Fain would he have come out to join his countrymen in arms at the commencement of the contest; but the peremptory order of his father enjoined his continuance in England, to prosecute his studies and finish his education. As a dutiful son, he obeyed these orders; but as a patriot burning with desire to defend his country, he dismissed Coke, Littleton, and all the tribe of jurists, and substituted in their place Vauban, Folard, and other writers on war. He also availed himself of the excellent opportunities which London affords of acquiring practical knowledge of the manual exercise, of tactics, and the mechanism of war. Thus instructed, as soon as he was a freeman of legal age, he quitted England for France, and by a circuitous voyage in neutral vessels, and at a considerable risk, made his way good, in the year 1777, to Charleston.

"Independence had been declared—the American army was raised, officered, and in the field. He who, by his attainments in general science, and particularly in the military art, deserved high rank, had no ordinary door left open to serve his country, but by entering in the lowest grade of an army abounding with officers. General Washington, ever attentive to merit, instantly took him into his family as a supernumerary aid-de-camp. Shortly after this appointment, he had an opportunity of indulging his military ardour. He fought and was wounded in the battle of Germantown, October 4th, 1777. He continued in General Washington's family, in the middle states, till the British had retreated from Philadelphia to New York, and was engaged in the battle of Monmouth, June 28, 1778.

"After this, the war being transferred more northwardly, he was indulged in attaching himself to the army on Rhode Island, where the most active operations were expected soon to take place. There he was entrusted with the command of some light troops. The bravery and good conduct which he displayed on this occasion was honoured by Congress.

"On the 5th of November, 1778, they resolved, 'that John Laurens, Esq. aid-de-camp to General Washington, be presented with a continental commission of lieutenant-colonel, in testimony of the sense which Congress entertain of his patriotic and spirited services as a volunteer in the American army; and of his brave conduct in several actions, particularly in that of Rhode Island, on the 29th of August last; and that General Washington be directed, whenever an opportunity shall offer, to give Lieutenant-Colonel Laurens command agreeable to his rank.' On the next day, a letter from Lieutenant-Colonel Laurens was read in Congress, expressing 'his gratitude for the unexpected honour which Congress was pleased to confer on him by the resolution passed the day before; and the high satisfaction it would have afforded him, could he have accepted it without injuring the rights of the officers in the line of the army, and doing an evident injustice to his colleagues in the family of the commander-in-chief—that having been a spectator of the convulsions occasioned in the army by disputes of rank, he held the tranquillity of it too dear to be instrumental in disturbing it, and therefore entreated Congress to suppress the resolve of yesterday, ordering him a commission of lieutenant-colonel, and to accept his sincere thanks for the intended honour.' In this relinquishment there was a victory gained by patriotism over self-love. Lieutenant-Colonel Laurens loved military fame and rank; but he loved his country more, and sacrificed the former to preserve the peace and promote the interest of the latter.

"In the next year the British directed their military operations chiefly against the most southern states. Lieutenant-Colonel John Laurens was induced by double motives to repair to Carolina. The post of danger was always the object of his preference. His native state was become the theatre of war. To its aid he repaired, and in May, 1779, with a party of light troops, had a skirmish with the British at Tulifinny. In endeavouring to obstruct their progress towards Charleston, he received a wound. This was no sooner cured than he rejoined the army, and was engaged in the unsuccessful attack on Savannah, on the 9th of October of the same year. To prepare for the defence of Charleston, the reduction of which was known to be contemplated by the British, was the next object of attention among the Americans. To this Colonel Laurens devoted all the energies of his active mind.

"In the progress of the siege, which commenced in 1780, the success of defensive operations became doubtful. Councils of war were frequent—several of the citizens were known to wish for a surrender, as a termination of their toils and dangers. In these councils, and on proper occasions, Colonel Laurens advocated the abandonment of the front lines, and to retire to new ones to be erected within the old ones, and to risk an assault. When these spirited measures were opposed on the suggestion that the inhabitants preferred a capitulation, he declared that he would direct his sword to the heart of the first citizen who would urge a capitulation against the opinion of the commander-in-chief.

" When his superior officers, convinced of the inefficacy of further resistance, were disposed to surrender on terms of capitulation, he yielded to the neccessity of the case, and became a prisoner of war. This reverse of fortune opened a new door for serving his country in a higher line than he ever yet had done. He was soon exchanged, and reinstated in a capacity for acting. In expediting his exchange, Congress had the ulterior view of sending him a special minister to Paris, that he might urge the necessity of a vigorous co-operation on the part of France with the United States against Great Britain. When this was proposed to Colonel Laurens, he recommended and urged that Colonel Alexander Hamilton should be employed in preference to himself. Congress adhered to their first choice.

"Colonel Laurens sailed for France in the latter end of 1780, and there, in conjunction with Dr. Franklin, and Count de Vergennes, and Marquis de Castries, arranged the plan of the campaign for 1781, which eventuated in the surrender of Lord Cornwallis, and finally in a termination of the war. Within six months from the day Colonel Laurens left America, he returned to it, and brought with him the concerted plan of combined operations. Ardent to rejoin the army, he was indulged with making a verbal report of his negotiations to Congress; and in three days set out to resume his place as one of the aids of Washington. The American and French army about this time commenced the siege of York Town. In the course of it, Colonel Laurens, as second in command, with his fellow-aid, Colonel Hamilton, assisted in storming and taking an advanced British redoubt, which expedited the surrender of Lord Cornwallis. The articles of capitulation were arranged by Colonel Laurens on behalf of the Americans

"Charleston and a part of South Carolina still remained in the power of the British. Colonel Laurens thought nothing done while any thing remained undone. He therefore, on the surrender of Lord Cornwallis, repaired to South Carolina, and joined the southern army commanded by General Greene. In the course of the summer of 1782, he caught a common fever, and was sick in bed when an expedition was undertaken against a party of the British, which had gone to Combakee to carry off rice. Colonel Laurens rose from his sick bed and joined his countrymen. While leading an advanced party, he received a shot, which, on the 27th of August, 1782, at the close of the war, put an end to his valuable life, in the 27th year of his age. His many virtues have been ever since the subject of eulogy, and his early fall, of national lamentation. The fourth of July seldom passes without a tribute to his memory."

THOMAS MIFFLIN,

MAJOR-GENERAL IN THE AMERICAN ARMY.

"Thomas Mifflin, a major-general in the American army during the revolutionary war, and governor of Pennsylvania, was born in the year 1744, of parents who were Quakers. His education was intrusted to the care of the Rev. Dr. Smith, with whom he was connected in habits of cordial intimacy and friendship for more than forty years. Active and zealous, he engaged early in opposition to the measures of the British parliament. He was a member of the first Congress, in 1774. He took arms, and was among the first officers commissioned on the organization of the continental army, being appointed quartermaster-general in August, 1775. For this offence he was read out of the society of Quakers. In 1777, he was very useful in animating the militia, and enkindling the spirit which seemed to have been damped. His sanguine disposition, and his activity, rendered him insensible to the value of that coolness and caution which were essential to the preservation of such an army as was then under the command of General Washington. In 1787, he was a member of the convention which framed the constitution of the United States, and his name is affixed to that instrument. In October, 1788, he succeeded Franklin as president of the supreme executive council of Pennsylvania, in which station he continued till October, 1790. In September, a constitution for this state was formed by a convention, in which he presided, and he was chosen the first governor. In 1794, during the insurrection in Pennsylvania, he employed, to the advantage of his country, the extraordinary powers of elocution with which he was endowed. The imperfection of the militia laws was compensated by his eloquence. He made a circuit through the lower counties, and, at different places, publicly addressed the militia on the crisis in the affairs of their country, and through his animating exhortations the state furnished the quota required. He was succeeded in the office of governor by Mr. M'Kean, at the close of the year 1799, and he died at Lancaster, January 20, 1800, in the fifty-seventh year of his age."

GILBERT MOTTIER LAFAYETTE.

Major-General of the American Army.

Marquis de Lafayette was born on the 6th of September, 1757, at the chateau de Chavagnac, in the department of Haute Loire, and was the inheritor of a princely fortune, and descended from distinguished ancestors. At seven years of age, he entered the college of Louis le Grande, at Paris, and commenced his literary education. Here the lovely but ill-fated Antoinette, the late queen of France, took him under her immediate patronage, and at a very early age, he rose to the rank of a commissioned officer in the king's guards. In 1774, he married the Countess de Noilles. At nineteen years of age, he sailed for America, and landed on the shores of South Carolina, This illustrious friend had become an advocate of the colonies, and felt all that ardor in the cause of liberty which did not desert him in maturer years. Lafayette had watched attentively the momentous controversy between Great Britain and her oppressed subjects, and resolved to make any sacrifice in their cause.

He made known his intention to Dr. Franklin then our commissioner in France, who laid before him the disastrous state of the country. "The more hopeless your cause," said he, "the more occasion is there for my assistance, the more honor shall I acquire by bestowing it." He immediately equipped a vessel for this enterprise at his own expense, and severing the ties which would have detained him in his native country, he sailed for the United States. Arrived at Philadelphia, he presented himself before Congress. "I am come," said he, "to request two favors of this assemblage of patriots. One is that I may serve in your army; the other, that I receive no pay." He was immediately received into the family of Washington, and congress, in July following, tendered him a commission of major-general. Soon after, learning the embarrassments of the army, he gave Washington 60,000 francs, (about 11,000 dollars,) to procure supplies; by which generous act, Washington was so affected, that he embraced Lafayette with tears of joy and affection. At the battle of Brandywine, the marquis exhibited full evidence of his bravery and military character, and in this bloody contest was wounded. After his recovery, he joined General Green, in New Jersey, and was at the head of 2000 men, whom he had formed, clothed, armed, equipped and disciplined himself. He was afterwards actively employed in different parts of the country, till 1779, when he returned to France, his object to obtain assistance for his adopted country. In this he succeeded, and in May, 1780, he returned with the joyful intelligence that a French fleet and army would soon arrive on our coast. He immediately resumed his command, and in the campaigns of 1780 and 1781, he displayed the most consummate generalship in preserving his little army, then opposed to Lord Cornwallis till the siege of that general at Yorktown, where, collected and undismayed, he shared largely in the honors of the day. In November, 1781, the contest, in which he had been so nobly engaged, drawing near a completion, Lafayette signified his intention of returning to his country. After the conclusion of peace, in August, 1784, General Lafayette again visited the United States, and several of the larger cities, in some of which the freedom of the city was presented him; he returned to France in December following.

General Lafayette was a member of the As

sembly of Notables at Versailles, in 1787, and in 1789 he was elected a member of the States General, made president of that assembly, and commandant of the National Guards. In this capacity his influence was exerted in favor of lenient measures; and he did much to prevent the mob of Paris from running into those horrid excesses which were afterwards committed. He acted a conspicuous part on the day the constitution was adopted, and soon after resigned his command. In 1792, he was called again into service; but on that memorable day, the 10th of August, when the royal family fled to the National Assembly for safety, he opposed the fury of the mob, was deprived of command, a price was set on his head, and he was obliged to fly his country for safety. He was thrown into prison by the king of Prussia, and afterwards chained and imprisoned by the emperor of Austria in the citadel at Olmutz. His estate was confiscated. In prison, he was subjected to the most barbarous treatment, and frequently threatened with an ignominious death. Great exertions were made to obtain his liberation without effect, until, in 1797, in settling terms of peace with Austria, Bonaparte expressly stipulated that Lafayette should be set at liberty, and in 1799, after the overthrow of the French Directory, he returned to France, and settled at La Grange, about forty miles from Paris. Previous to Bonaparte's first abdication, he was elected to the chamber of deputies, and there proposed a vote of permanent session, which was passed, and in consequence, the emperor found himself under the necessity of abdicating the throne. From that period to the time of his embarkation for the United States, with the exception of his having been once again elected to the chamber of deputies, General Lafayette spent most of his time in the pursuits of agriculture at La Grange.

As soon as it was known in the United States that the Marquis Lafayette had once more embarked for the shores of his adopted country, a general joy pervaded the nation, and all classes of citizens were prepared to take a lively interest in his arrival. The cities of New York and Boston particularly, anticipated the event with some degree of impatience, and entered into such general arrangements for his reception as were best calculated to do honor to themselves and their illustrious guest.

General Lafayette, accompanied by his son George Washington Lafayette, Mr. Auguste La

Vasseur, and one servant, arrived in the harbor of New York, on the morning of the 15th of August, in the ship Cadmus, Captain Allyn, after a pleasant passage of thirty-one days from Havre. His arrival was made known by the telegraph at an early hour, and spread through the city with electrical rapidity. Broadway was soon thronged, and the Battery crowded with people, who sallied forth with the expectation that the hero and veteran of two revolutions would come directly to the city. The arrangements of the city authorities, however, for his reception, having been seasonably communicated to him, he landed at Staten Island, and was conducted to the seat of the Vice-President, where he remained through the day, and passed the night. Fort Lafayette fired a salute as the ship passed, and a salute was fired as the general landed.

In the city the national flag was immediately hoisted and displayed at all the public places during the day.

PROCEEDINGS, UPON RECEPTION OF THE MARQUIS LAFAYETTE INTO THE CITY OF NEW YORK, ON MONDAY THE 16TH OF AUGUST.

Arrangements of the Corporation.

The committee of arrangements of the corporation have the pleasure to announce to their fellow-citizens the arrival of the distinguished guest of their country, the Marquis de Lafayette.

The following are the arrangements made for his reception in the city.

The committee of arrangements of the Corporation, the generals and other officers of the United States Army, the officers of the Navy, the major-generals and the brigadier-generals of the Militia, the president of the Chamber of Commerce, the committee from the Society of Cincinnati, will proceed at 9 o'clock this day to Staten Island, where the marquis is lodged, and escort him to the city. They will be accompanied by the steam-boats, all with decorations except that in which the marquis is embarked, which will only have the flag of the United States and the flag of New York; bands of music being in each.

The marquis' embarkation will be announced by a salute from Fort Lafayette and the steamship Robert Fulton.

The forts in the harbor will also salute as the vessels pass.

The masters of vessels are requested to hoist their flags at mast-head, and, where convenien to dress their vessels.

The bells of the city will be rung from 12 to 1 o'clock.

The portrait room of the City Hall is appropriated to the marquis, where, during his stay, he will, after this day, between the hours of twelve and two o'clock, receive the visits of such of the citizens as are desirous of paying their respects to him.

The committee of arrangements of the Corporation having accepted the proffered services of the steam-ship Robert Fulton, and the steamboats Chancellor Livingston, Oliver Ellsworth, Henry Eckford, Connecticut, Bellona, Olive Branch, Nautilus, &c.; they were all superbly dressed with flags and streamers of every nation, and directed to meet and form an aquatic escort between the south part of the Battery and Governor's Island, and thence proceed in order to Staten Island. The spectacle, as the boats were assembling, was truly interesting and beautiful. The Battery was crowded with respectable people of both sexes; Castle Garden was filled, and every boat that arrived to take its station was completely crowded with elegantly dressed ladies and gentlemen. The appearance of the Robert Fulton, as she came down the East River, from the Navy Yard, escorted by the Connecticut and Oliver Ellsworth, all superbly decorated, was rich beyond description. Her yards were manned to the round-tops, with about 200 seamen from the Constitution, who made an elegant appearance; and a battalion of marines, under the command of Major Smith, was on board, with a band of music, and many of the naval officers upon this station, together with several ladies and private gentlemen.

Arrived at the place of rendezvous, the several vessels comprising the fleet took their station, and proceeded in regular order to the quarantine, as follows:—First, the Chancellor Livingston, on board of which were the committee of the Corporation, Major-General Morton and suite, a number of the members of the Cincinnati, including Colonels Willet, Varick, Trumbull, Platt, and others, together with a few ladies, several officers and professors from West Point, accompanied by the excellent military band attached to that institution. On the right of the Chancellor, and about a length in rear, was the Connecticut, and on the left, to correspond, was the Oliver Ellsworth. Directly in the rear of the Chancellor was the Robert Fulton, whose lofty masts and widespread arms, which literally swarmed with men towered proudly above her less-pretending, but not less gay and beautiful consorts. On the right of the Robert Fulton, about a length in the rear, was the Bellona, and on the left, the Henry Eckford, in a station to correspond; and the squadron was closed by the Olive Branch and Nautilus. The signals exchanged, and the steam-boats having attained their stations, as above stated, the squadron got under way, amidst the cheers of thousands of delighted spectators. The view of this fleet will perhaps never be forgotten. It was not only unique, but beyond a doubt, one of the most splendid spectacles ever witnessed on this part of the globe. The squadron, bearing six thousand of our fellow-citizens, majestically took its course towards Staten Island, there to take on board our long expected and honored guest. At one o'clock the fleet arrived at Staten Island, and in a few minutes a landau was seen approaching the hotel, near the ferry. The Marquis, the Vice-President, and the Ex-Governor Ogden of New Jersey, having alighted, a procession was formed, and the venerable stranger, supported by these gentlemen, followed by all the officers of the island, and a crowd of citi zens, passed through a triumphal arch, round which was tastefully entwined the French and American colors. As soon as the marquis and suite entered on the broad stairs, connected with, and leading to, the steam-boat which was to convey him to the city, he was received by the committee of the Common Council, who conducted him on board the Chancellor Livingston. On entering this splendid vessel, the marines paid him military honors. He was now introduced to the committees from most of our honored associations, and the general officers representing the infantry. The West Point band all this time was playing " See the Conquering Hero Comes," "*Ou peut on etre mieux*," "Hail Columbia," and the "Marseilles Hymn." The steamship now fired a salute, and the whole squadron got under way for the city, in the same order as before, except that the Bellona and Olive Branch fastened each side of the Cadmus, (the ship which brought the general from France,) decorated with colors, and filled with passengers, majestically moved up the bay. The sea was smooth and placid, and the breeze cool and agreeable. The most interesting sight was the reception of the general by his old companions in arms,

Colonel Marinus Willet, now in his eighty-fifth year, General Van Courtland, General Clarkson, and the other worthies whom we have mentioned. Colonel Fish, General Lewis, and several of his comrades were absent. He embraced them all affectionately, and Colonel Willet again and again. He knew and remembered them all. It was a reünion of a long separated family.

After the ceremony of embracing and congratulations were over, he sat down alongside of Colonel Willet, who grew young again, and fought all his battles o'er. "Do you remember," said he, "at the battle of Monmouth, I was volunteer aid to General Scott? I saw you in the heat of battle. You were but a boy, but you were a serious and sedate lad. Aye, aye; I remember well. And on the Mohawk, I sent you fifty Indians, and you wrote me that they set up such a yell, that they frightened the British horse, and they ran one way and the Indians another."

No person who witnessed this interview will ever forget it; many an honest tear was shed on the occasion. The young men retired to a little distance, while the venerable soldiers were indulging recollections, and embracing each other again and again; and the surrounding youth silently dropt the tear they could no longer restrain. Such sincere, such honest feelings were never more plainly or truly expressed. The sudden changes of the countenance of the marquis plainly evinced the emotions he endeavored to suppress. He manfully supported this truly trying situation for some time, when a revolutionary story from the venerable Willet recalled circumstances long past: the incident, the friend alluded to, made the marquis sigh, and his swelling heart was relieved when he burst into tears. The sympathetic feelings extended to all present; and even the hardy tar rubbed away the tear he could no longer restrain. The scene was too affecting to be continued, and one of the Cincinnati, anxious to divert the attention of the marquis, his eyes flowing with tears, announced the near approach of the steam-ship. The marquis advanced to the quarter-railing, where he was no sooner perceived by the multitude, than an instantaneous cheer most loudly expressed the delight they experienced. The other steamboats in succession presented themselves, and passed, each giving three enthusiastic cheers. The marquis was delighted, and especially with the activity and quickness with which 200 of our gallant seamen manned the yards of the steam-frigate, previous to the salute. About two o'clock, P. M., the fleet arrived off the Battery. What an impressive scene!—3000 men, making a splendid appearance, formed in line with a battering train. The ramparts and parapets of the Castle were lined with ladies and gentlemen. The flagstaff, the windows, and even the roofs of the houses facing the bay, were literally crowded with spectators. Hundreds of boats and wherries surrounded the Battery. The marquis left the Chancellor Livingston in a barge commanded by Lieutenant Mix, of the navy, accompanied by the committee of the Corporation, and the Cincinnati, the generals of infantry, &c.; and landed amidst the cheers and acclamations of 30,000 people, who filled the Castle, Battery, and surrounding grounds within sight. The marquis now entered the Castle, which was tastefully carpeted from the landing place to the receiving rooms. He then partook of some refreshment, and was introduced to some distinguished citizens. Perceiving the restless anxiety of nearly 3000 persons in the Castle, to see the general, the marquis advanced to the centre of the rear of the Castle, and was greeted with loud cheers. From Castle Garden, he proceeded with the appointed committee, and the military and naval officers, to review the line of troops under the command of Brigadier-General Benedict. The muster was, on this occasion, unusually numerous and splendid, each corps vying with the others in paying a tribute of respect to the soldier of the revolution, the friend and companion of Washington. After the review, the general, accompanied by General Morton, entered a barouche, drawn by four horses.

The committee of the Corporation, accompanied by the general's son, George Washington Lafayette, and his secretary, Mr. Le Vasseur, followed the carriages. The general was escorted by a corps of cavalry, and at the head of the column of troops, proceeded up Broadway to the City Hall. The crowds which had assembled to pay honor to the respected visitor, and to be gratified with a view of his person, were such as almost to prevent the passage of the carriages and the troops. The scene could not but have afforded to the general the most delightful gratification. The houses to the very roofs were filled with spectators, and to the incessant cheers of the multitude, graceful females signified their welcome by the silent, but not less grateful and affecting testimony of the waving of handkerchiefs.

Arrived at the City Hall, the marquis was conducted by the committee to the Common Council Chamber, where the Corporation were assembled. The members of the Common Council rose on his entrance, and upon being presented by the chairman, Alderman Zabriskie, to the Mayor, his honor addressed him in the following speech:

Address of the Mayor.

"General—In the name of the municipal authority of the city, I bid you a sincere welcome to the shores of a country, of whose fredom and happiness you will ever be considered one of the most honored and beloved founders.

"Your only contemporaries in arms, of whom indeed but few remain, have not forgot, and their posterity will never forget, the *young and gallant Frenchman* who consecrated his youth, his talents, his fortune, and his exertions, to their cause—who exposed his life—who shed his blood, that they might become free and happy. They will recollect with profound emotion, so long as they remain worthy of the liberties they enjoy, and of the exertions you made to obtain them, that you came to them in the darkest period of their struggle — that you linked your fortune with theirs, when it seemed almost hopeless — that you shared in the dangers, privations and sufferings of that bitter struggle, nor quitted them for a moment till it was consummated on the glorious field of Yorktown. Half a century has passed since that great event, and in that time your name has become as dear to the friends, and as inseparably connected with the cause of freedom in the old, as in the new world.

"The people of the United States look up to you as to one of their most honored parents — the country cherishes you as one of the most beloved of her sons. I hope and trust, sir, that not only the present, but future conduct of my countrymen, to the latest period of time, will, among other slanders, refute the unjust imputation that republics are always ungrateful to their benefactors.

"In behalf of my fellow-citizens of New York, and speaking the warm and universal sentiments of the whole people of the United States I repeat their welcome to our common country

"Permit me to add, that the moment of my life to which I shall look back with the greatest pleasure and pride, will be that in which it fell to my lot to be an organ for expressing, however feebly, a nation's gratitude."

General Lafayette's Answer.

"Sir,—While I am so affectionately received by the citizens of New York and their worthy representatives, I feel myself overwhelmed with inexpressible emotions. The sight of the American shore, after so long an absence; the recollection of the many respected friends and dear companions, no more to be found on this land; the pleasure to recognize those who have survived; this immense concourse of a free republican population, who so kindly welcome me; the admirable appearance of the troops; the presence of a corps of the national navy;—have excited sentiments, to which no human language can be adequate. You have been pleased, sir, to allude to the happiest times, the unalloyed enjoyments of my public life. It is the pride of my heart to have been one of the earliest adopted sons of America: I am proud also to add, that upwards of forty years ago I have been particularly honored with the freedom of this city. I beg you, Mr. Mayor,—I beg you, gentlemen, to accept yourselves, and to transmit to the citizens of New York, the homage of my profound and everlasting gratitude, devotion and respect."

The general and his son were then introduced to the members of the Common Council individually.

After the adjournment of the Common Council, the marquis received the marching salute in front of the City Hall, and again entered the hall, accompanied by his son and suite, and in the governor's room received the Society of the Cincinnati, composed of his surviving brothers and companions in the field, a small number of whom still remain to meet and congratulate their long absent, but highly respected friend and fellow-soldier. Here, also, he was met by the officers of the army and navy, and many citizens and strangers. From the hall, he was accompanied by the Common Council, and many distinguished persons, to the City Hotel, to dine, escorted by the troops.

The whole exhibition, from the landing at the Battery to the time of the dispersion of the people at the Park, was in a high degree interesting and gratifying. The numbers collected were perhaps unequalled on any former festive occasion. The houses through Broadway were filled with spectators of the first respectability, and the street was crowded with people. Every expression of good feeling was manifested from the windows, doors, and side-walks; the stranger was welcomed with unfeigned cordiality; and we think it must have afforded to the marquis an unusual degree of delight to find that his services were remembered and acknowledged, and his name cherished, by a free and grateful people.

The day was singularly fine — the water scene exceeded in splendor and effect anything of the kind that has ever been exhibited here; the appearance of the military was highly creditable in equipments, movements and discipline; and we have not a doubt their appearance, when contrasted by his recollection with the suffering troops of the war of independence, must have made a deep impression upon his mind.

On Wednesday morning, the 18th, in compliance with an invitation from Captain Rodgers, commandant of the Navy Yard, General Lafayette, attended by the committee of arrangements, and a select circle of ladies and gentlemen, proceeded, in the elegant steamboat Chancellor Kent, to visit the Navy Yard at Brooklyn.

As the James Kent passed the Grampus lying in the North River, a salute of 21 guns was fired.

The Kent then proceeded round the Battery and up the East River, until she came to anchor at the dock, where the steam-frigate is moored, when the marquis and the ladies and gentlemen of the party disembarked — the United States frigate Constellation firing at the same time a salute of 21 guns. On landing, he was received by three cheers from 200 sailors drawn up for the occasion.

The general then went on board of the steam-frigate, and was much pleased with the construction of this formidable and unique naval battlement.

On returning, the jolly tars gave three more hearty cheers, and the general proceeded in a barge to the Navy Yard; when another salute of 21 guns was fired on his landing, and he was received by a battalion of marines.

The general was then conducted on board the Washington 74, where refreshments were provided for the whole party. After refreshing himself, the general took a rapid survey of the ships, and those now building, and returned on board the Kent, when another salute was fired by the Constitution.

Upon the return of the Marquis Lafayette from the Navy Yard on Wednesday, he was introduced, with his son, to the Historical Society, at their room in the Institution, at two o'clock, P. M. According to a resolution passed the day before, they were made members of the society.

After the marquis' arrival at New York, he early announced his intention to visit Boston, where he had been particularly invited by distinguished individuals, and by the city authority; especially as the commencement at the university in Cambridge, the literary jubilee of the state, was to be celebrated in a few days. While in New York, he received invitations from Philadelphia, Albany, New Haven, Hartford, and some other cities, to make a visit to those places, but his desire was first to visit Boston, if possible.

The interesting visit at New York being closed, at an early hour on Friday morning, a scene of general bustle and activity commenced, preparatory to the departure of the general for

Boston. The city corporation had provided an elegant carriage to accommodate him on his journey to Boston, and deputed four of their number to attend him on his route.

He was too sensible of the sincerity and warmth of their felicitation, not to delay his journey at several villages, and to reciprocate their kind and cordial salutations. It was nearly midnight when he reached the town of Dedham, about ten miles from Boston. Most of the houses in this pleasant village were handsomely illuminated; and a great number of the inhabitants of both sexes were assembled to greet him. During the short stay he was able to make here, he was introduced to many of the principal citizens of the town and vicinity, who had been anticipating his arrival for some hours. When he passed through Roxbury, at one o'clock, he was accompanied by a large cavalcade of citizens of that place and from Boston; and a salute was fired by the Roxbury corps of artillery. His arrival here was also announced by the ascent of rockets from an eminence in the centre of the town; and the note of preparation was thus given for the parade and pleasure of the succeeding day, which had been anticipated with uncommon interest and delight. Lafayette and suite proceeded to the mansion of his Excellency the Governor, to which they had been invited; and the meeting between them was truly affectionate and cordial.

On Tuesday the 24th, the inhabitants of Boston hailed the morning light with peculiar emotions, and were abroad at an early hour, preparing for the general testimonies of gratitude and respect to be presented to the "nation's guest." Many of the older citizens recollected him in his youthful days, when he visited the town. *forty-six* years ago, at the request of Congress and Washington, to prevail on the French admiral to coöperate with his fleet in a contemplated attack upon the British forces at Rhode Island. They had not forgotten his zeal and ardor in the cause of America. They knew his great attachment to, and respect for, the *immortal* chief of the American army, and the confidence which Washington cherished for Lafayette. And all classes, without intending to lessen the preëminent services and virtues of Washington, who, under Providence, was the great and chief agent in achieving our independence, and in preserving it, after it had been once established — or to undervalue

.he important efforts and courage of many other revered heroes and patriots, too numerous to be here named;—all, all were eager to join in the spontaneous offering of gratitude and affection, to one so justly celebrated and so *greatly beloved.*

He entered the city, the capital of the state, about eleven o'clock; and his reception was a triumph and a jubilee. The day was as bright as his laurels, and as mild as his virtues. The various bodies designated to compose the procession, and perform the honors of the day, assembled at an early hour. The cavalcade was formed in Common street, at nine o'clock. It was very numerous, and consisted of the citizens of Boston, of all ranks and classes, on horseback. Proceeding to the extreme southern part of the city, near the line of Roxbury, they were joined by the Mayor and Aldermen, and members of the Common Council, the Society of Cincinnati, a great number of public civil characters, and strangers of distinction, all in carriages; by the General and Field Officers of the first division of militia, and officers of the army and navy of the United States. An innumerable concourse of people on foot lined the s de-walks of the spacious street where the procession was to be formed, the entrance to the city from Roxbury, and fortunately named WASHINGTON STREET. The cavalcade then proceeded to the mansion of Governor Eustis, which is a short distance within the town of Roxbury, and escorted General Lafayette and suite to the line, where the city authorities and others, who were to compose the procession, were in waiting to receive him. Here he was greeted by the immense assemblage of citizens with repeated and enthusiastic acclamations, for several minutes, when the mayor welcomed him with much feeling, in the following speech : —

" Sir, — The citizens of Boston welcome you on your return to the United States ; mindful of your early zeal in the cause of American Independence, grateful for your distinguished share in the perils and glories of its achievements. When, urged by a generous sympathy, you first landed on these shores, you found a people engaged in an arduous and eventful struggle for liberty, with apparently inadequate means, and amidst dubious omens. After a lapse of nearly half a century, you find the same people prosperous beyond all hope and all precedent, their liberty secure; sitting in its strength; without fear and without reproach.

"In your youth you joined the standard of three millions of people, raised in an unequal and uncertain conflict. In your advanced age you return and are met by ten millions of people, their descendants, whose hearts throng hither to greet your approach and rejoice in it.

"This is not the movement of a turbulent populace, excited by the fresh laurels of some recent conqueror; it is a grave, moral, intellectual impulse.

"A whole people in the enjoyment of freedom, as perfect as the condition of our nature permits, recur with gratitude, increasing with the daily increasing sense of their blessings, to the memory of those, who, by their labors and in their blood, laid the foundation of our liberties.

"Your name, sir,—the name of Lafayette, is associated with the most perilous and most glorious periods of our Revolution;—with the imperishable names of Washington, and of that numerous host of heroes which adorn the proudest archives of American history, and are engraven in indelible traces on the hearts of the whole American people.

"Accept then, sir, in the sincere spirit in which it is offered, this simple tribute to your virtues.

"Again, sir, the citizens of Boston bid you welcome to the cradle of American Independence, and to scenes consecrated with the blood shed by the earliest martyrs in its cause."

General Lafayette then rose in his carriage, and in a most interesting manner replied as follows:—

"The emotions of love and gratitude, which I have been accustomed to feel on my entering this city, have ever mingled with a sense of religious reverence for the cradle of *American*, and let me hope it will hereafter be said, of *universal* liberty.

"What must be, sir, my feelings, at the blessed moment, when, after so long an absence, I find myself again surrounded by the good citizens of Boston — where I am so affectionately, so honorably welcomed, not only by old friends, but by several successive generations; where I can witness the prosperity, the immense improvements, that have been the just reward of a noble struggle, virtuous morals, and truly republican institutions.

"I beg you, Mr. Mayor, gentlemen of the

City Council, and all of you, beloved citizens of Boston, to accept the respectful and warm thanks of a heart which has for nearly half a century been particularly devoted to your illustrious city."

The reply of the general was received with new plaudits of the assembled people; and "Welcome, welcome, Lafayette! friend of Washington! friend of America! friend of Liberty!" was repeated again and again; and the heights of Dorchester and Roxbury echoed with the joyful acclamation.

The procession was then formed, and passed through Washington, Milk, Broad, State, Court, and Tremont streets, to Boylston street, adjoining the south part of the Common, in the following order:— Three marshals, the Boston corps of Light Dragoons, a battalion of Light Infantry, composed of the Fusiliers, Boston Light Infantry, Winslow Blues, Washington Light Infantry, New England Guards, Rangers, and City Guards; and a full band of music. Then followed the chief marshal, attended by aids; members of the City Council, Committee of Arrangements, the President of the Common Council, and senior Alderman, all in carriages. Here was placed another marshal, immediately preceding the elegant barouche, drawn by four beautiful white horses, in which rode the distinguished guest of the city and of the nation, accompanied by the mayor, with marshals also on either side. The son and friend of Lafayette, and gentlemen aldermen from New York, next followed in carriages; and these were succeeded by the Society of the Cincinnati, public characters, judges and legislators, and distinguished strangers, in carriages also. Immediately after, two marshals; field and staff officers of the militia, mounted on horseback, and followed also by two marshals. The cavalcade of citizens, of all ranks and in great numbers, with marshals attending, closed the voluntary but triumphant procession.

The dwelling-houses and stores on the streets through which the procession was conducted, were crowded with inhabitants in every part. The ladies thus situated caught the enthusiasm of the occasion, waved their white handkerchiefs, and with smiles and gladness, greeted the veteran hero, who appeared affected and delighted by these demonstrations of a joyful welcome.

Excepting the cavalcade, the procession

passed through the Common from Boylston to Park street, on the eastern margin, and between two lines of children, of both sexes, belonging to the several schools in the city. Their ages were from about eight to twelve, and nearly three thousand in number. Their dress was neat and uniform; the misses in white, and the masters in white pantaloons and blue spencers. They also wore ribbons on their breasts, stamped with a miniature likeness of Lafayette. As the carriage in which the general rode was passing, one of the misses darted from the line where she was standing, and requested to speak with him. She was handed into the carriage, and by the mayor presented to Lafayette, who pressed an affectionate kiss on her blooming, yet blushing cheek. She had confidence, however, to address him, and place a wreath of flowers which she held on his head. He made a short but affectionate reply, and placed the wreath on the seat of the carriage. Attached to the wreath of flowers was a small piece of paper, carefully folded, which contained these lines, said to be composed by the mother of the child:

'An infant hand presents these blushing flowers,
Glowing and pure as childhood's artless hours,

Where roses bloom, and buds of *promise* smile
Repaying with their charms the culturer's toil.

Oh! *take them*, FATHER, they were culled *for you!*
(Still bright with warm *affection's* sacred dew —)
O let them live in thy benignant smile,
And o'er thy *brow of glory* bloom awhile!

Twined with the *laurel* Fame on thee bestowed,
When thy young heart with patriot ardor glowed;
Self-exiled from the charms of *wealth* and *love*,
And *home*, and *friends*, thou didst *our champion prove*,
And, by the side of glorious WASHINGTON,
Didst make our grateful country *all thine own!*

Go, fragile offering, speak the ardent joy
Our bosoms feel, which time can ne'er destroy!"

Arches were thrown across several of the principal streets through which Lafayette was conducted, covered with evergreens and flowers, and containing appropriate mottos. There were two in Washington street. On one of these was very legibly written, "1776—WASHINGTON and LAFAYETTE. *Welcome, Lafayette—A Republic not ungrateful.*" On the other,—

"WELCOME, LAFAYETTE."

"The fathers in glory shall sleep,
   Who gathered with thee to the fight;
But the sons will eternally keep
   The tablet of gratitude bright.

> We bow not the neck,
>   And we bend not the knee,
> But our hearts, LAFAYETTE,
>   We surrender to thee."

When the procession arrived at the steps of the State House, near the head of Park street, salutes were fired by a battalion of artillery, on the eminence on the western part of the Common, and at the Navy Yard at Charlestown. Salutes were also fired by a battalion of artillery, placed on the heights of Dorchester, (now South Boston,) when General Lafayette reached the line of the city, at eleven o'clock.

The Governor and Executive Council of the Commonwealth were assembled in the spacious Senate Chamber to receive Lafayette in the name of the representatives of the people, and in pursuance of their resolve of June preceding, as well as in accordance with their own personal feelings and wishes. His Excellency the Governor here addressed him with great feeling,* in the following concise and pertinent speech:—

---

* Governor Eustis was so affected that he had to call on one of his aids to read a greater part of the address.

"Sir, our Friend,—In the name of the government, and in behalf of the citizens of Massachusetts, I have the honor to greet you with a cordial and affectionate welcome.

"We thank God that he has been pleased to preserve you through the scenes of peril and of suffering which have distinguished your patriotic and eventful life, and that we are indulged with this occasion of renewing to you our grateful acknowledgments for the important services which you have rendered to our common country.

"In the last surviving major-general of the American revolutionary army we recognize a benefactor and friend, from a distant and gallant nation; who, inspired by love of liberty, subjected himself in his youth to the toils and hazards of a military life, in support of our rights. Under our illustrious Washington, you were instrumental in establishing the liberties of our country, while your gallantry in the field secured to yourself an imperishable renown.

"With the enjoyment of the blessings of independence, we shall never cease to associate the name of Lafayette, and our prayer to Heaven will be for his health and prosperity."

To which the general, with much animation, replied:—

"Sir,—When, in the name of the people and government of this state, your excellency is pleased so kindly to welcome an American veteran, I am proud to share the enjoyments of such a reception with my revolutionary companions and brother soldiers. Sir, I am delighted with what I see, I am oppressed with what I feel; but I depend upon you, as an old friend, to do justice to my sentiments."

Afterwards, a great number of gentlemen were introduced to Lafayette, in the Senate Chamber; of whom were the judges and other public officers of the United States, of the state and of the city; members of the Society of Cincinnati, with their venerable and distinguished president, Honorable John Brooks, late Governor of the Commonwealth. Lafayette recognized his old military and personal friend at the first sight, and embraced him with great cordiality and affection. Some other veterans of the revolutionary army, who were present, he also recollected, and discovered strong emotions as they approached him and took his hand. Indeed, he was so eager to meet them, that he very generally first seized them, and clung to them with all the affection of a brother. The scene was inexpressibly affecting. There was not a heart untouched—not a cheek unmoistened by the falling tear. To weep then was not weakness; it was proof of gratitude and of a generous feeling, which is an honor to human nature.

By particular request, and to gratify the wishes of the people collected in front of the State House, General Lafayette appeared in the colonnade of this superb edifice, where he was greeted with loud and continued cheers. He was then conducted by the committee of arrangements to the residence provided for him at the head of Park street. A public dinner was given by the city authorities, in honor of their noble guest; and the invitation was extended to senators and members of congress the governor and ex-governor of the Commonwealth, judicial, and other public characters.

While in Boston, invitations flowed in, and hospitalities were tendered to him, from all parts of New England. The general, ever anxious to please and gratify the people in all sections of the United States, improved his earliest convenience to visit in course most of the principal cities and towns in the New England States, closing his first Eastern tour the 1st of September, at Hartford, where he embarked on board a magnificently decorated steamboat which floated tranquilly over the sound, and landed him again safely at New York, amid the welcoming shouts of the united voices of the citizens of the empire city of the Union.

After another short visit in New York, Lafayette again left by steamboat up the Hudson, for West Point, Albany, and intermediate places, at which points it is deemed unnecessary to state that impatient thousands waited to welcome the nation's guest.

The general made but a short stay at the places above named, when he again returned down the Hudson to New York, where he arrived safely at Courtlandt-street wharf. Lafayette was here again literally overwhelmed with hospitalities tendered from all quarters, and at almost every step the welkin rang with "cheers" and "welcomes" which testified to him how dear he was in the hearts of a nation of freemen.

The general again rested himself a few days, on this his third visit at New York, after which he left on his triumphal march through New Jersey, Delaware, Pennsylvania and Maryland on to the city of Washington,—the seat of that government for which his youthful heart had inspired him to do so much, in assisting to lay its corner-stone.

Lafayette was escorted into the capitol, passed through the rotunda, and entered the Tent of Washington. Here he was met by the mayor, and other authorities, officers, clergy, &c., &c. In the course of his reply to an address from the mayor, full of fine feeling, the general said:—

"Among the circumstances of my life to which you have been pleased to allude, none can afford me such dear recollections as my having been early adopted as an American soldier; so there is not a circumstance of my reception in which I take so much pride, as in sharing those honors with my beloved companions in arms.

"Happy I am to feel that the marks of affection and esteem bestowed on me, bear testimony to my perseverance in the American principles I received under the tent of Washington, and of which I shall, to my latest breath, prove myself a devoted disciple.

"I beg you, Mr. Mayor, and the gentlemen of the Corporation, to accept my respectful acknowledgements to you and to the citizens of Washington."

After the customary introductions, the general, accompanied by the mayor, and attended by General Brown, and Commodore Tingey, proceeded to the President's house, where the President advanced to him, and gave him a cordial and affectionate reception.

The interview was a most impressive one, surrounded as he was by all the members of the cabinet, and a large number of the officers of the army and navy, who waited to welcome one of the nation's benefactors.

It rarely happens that official robes and military armor find a more fitting occasion for display. It is meet they should bow to disinterested benevolence.

After a few minutes of interchange of courtesies, the general took his leave, and retired to his quarters at Gadsby's hotel.

Lafayette passed two or three days in Washington, visiting President Monroe again, as also the Secretaries of State, of the Treasury, and of War, and Major-General Brown of the United States Army.

On Thursday, the 15th of October, the general rode over to Georgetown, and Friday, by invitation, he visited the Navy Yard, and on Saturday proceeded on his visit to Alexandria and Yorktown. At Alexandria, he was received by the mayor, the Common Council, his brother masons and others. In the evening, the public buildings and many private houses were brilliantly illuminated. On the Sabbath, General Lafayette proceeded to Mount Vernon, and visited the tomb of Washington, his revered father and friend. While here, he was presented, by Mr. Custis, with a ring containing a portion of the hair of the sainted hero, together with the masonic sash and jewel formerly belonging to the great mason. In the course of a very eloquent address to the general on this occasion, Mr. Custis said: " Our fathers witnessed the dawn of your glory, partook of its meridian splendor; and oh, let their children enjoy the benign radiance of your setting sun. And when it shall sink in the horizon of nature, here, *here*, with pious duty, we will form your sepulchre; and, united in death as in life, by the side of the great chief you will rest in peace, till the last trump awakes the slumbering world, and calls your virtues to their great reward.

" The joyous shouts of millions of freemen

hailed your returning foot-print on our sands The arms of millions are opened wide to take you to their grateful hearts; and the prayers of millions ascend to the throne of the Eternal, that the choicest blessings of Heaven may cheer the latest days of Lafayette."

General Lafayette, after the sublime scenes at Washington and vicinity, proceeded down the Potomac, by special invitation, to visit Yorktown, Williamsburg, Norfolk, Petersburg and Richmond. The general left Richmond, November 2d, on a visit to his illustrious friend, Mr. Jefferson, and arrived at Monticello on Thursday, November 4th, when he was received by Mr. Jefferson, in a most feeling manner. They flew into each other's arms by a most cordial impulse, and remained locked in silent embrace for several minutes before their feelings could find utterance.

Lafayette passed a week at Monticello, to enjoy the repose of that beautiful seat, under the courteous hospitalities of his beloved friend, Jefferson.

From here the general left, with regret, on his return to Washington, where he arrived on Tuesday, the 23d day of November While here, a vote of the Senate was passed, inviting him to take a seat as one of their body to which he consented, and on entering the Senate Chamber, he was received with that august body standing.

During his stay in Washington at this time, a bill passed both houses of Congress, granting the general 200,000 dollars, and an entire township of land, to be located on any of the public lands that remain unsold.

General Lafayette commenced his tour from Washington through the Southern and Western States, about the 1st of March. In his course, he visited the principal towns in the States of North and South Carolina, Georgia. Alabama, Louisiana, Mississippi, Tennessee Missouri, Kentucky, Illinois and Ohio.

He visited Pittsburg, and returned to Albany by way of Buffalo. From Albany he proceeded directly to Boston, where he arrived on the 16th of June.

The compiler regrets that the limits of this work will not permit him to give a detailed account of this whole great tour; suffice it to say that the same military parades, civic feasts, cordial and affectionate addresses, triumphal arches and soldiers' tears, greeted Lafayette throughout a distance of more than 4000 miles.

These were not the momentary triumphs of a conqueror, fresh from the field of carnage, with blood-stained armor, and the echoing air of the stirring drum-beat; but the spontaneous outpouring of the hearts of other generations, who rise up to bless the patriot hero and benefactor of their country, who took their fathers by the hand, and was ready to lay down his life for their sake, and when he had given them an exalted rank among the nations of the earth, laid his laurels at their feet, and left them to the enjoyments of freedom, happiness and honor.

More than 3000 miles of the western tour of Lafayette was a pathless wilderness at the close of the revolution; now they can boast of nearly a dozen states, dotted all over with a free, virtuous, and intelligent population.

The sublime realities of this whole scene, when taken collectively, surpass the powers of pen or pencil. Altogether, it combines to make the history of Lafayette the most remarkable, save that of Washington, on record.

Time cannot dim the recollection of, or the

vast obligation to which we are under to, the great patriot, Lafayette.

After the general had made a complete tour through the United States, being received everywhere with the highest marks of gratitude which a free people could bestow, he sailed again for his native country, on the 7th of September, 1825, in a ship fitted out by government for that purpose, and called the Brandywine, in honor of his bravery in that memorable battle. He had a pleasant voyage, and arrived again in safety, the following month, in his own dear France; when he retired to the sweet fields of La Grange, where, during the agricultural months, he spent his time in directing the labors of his farm.

Lafayette passed the winters in Paris, and, during his stay there, in 1834, in riding for exercise, he exposed himself too much to the sudden changes of atmosphere, by which he took a sudden cold, and through which disease gave strong battle with the aged hero. Doctor Giron, with other eminent physicians, did all that the profession could do, but the aged general had not constitution enough to bear him through. He lingered along a few weeks, without much apparent suffering when his eyes turned upwards from a world *for* which he had done so much, to the gates of that heavenly heritage, the glory and enjoyments of which we trust he is in full participation.

Thus set the sun of one of the most remarkable heroes of modern times.

DECLARATION OF INDEPENDENCE.

WHEN, in the course of human events, it becomes necessary for one people to dissolve the political bands which have connected them with another, and to assume, among the powers of the earth, the separate and equal station to which the laws of nature and of nature's God entitle them, a decent respect to the opinions of mankind requires that they should declare the causes which impel them to the separation.

We hold these truths to be self-evident: that all men are created equal; that they are endowed by their Creator with certain unalienable rights; that among these are life, liberty and the pursuit of happiness; that, to secure these rights, governments are instituted among men, deriving their just powers from the consent of the governed; and that, whenever any form of government becomes destructive of these ends, it is the right of the people to alter or abolish it, and to institute new government, laying its foundations on such principles, and organizing its powers in such form, as to them shall seem most likely to effect their safety and happiness. Prudence, indeed, will dictate that governments long established should not be changed for light and transient causes; and, accordingly, all experience hath shown that mankind are more disposed to suffer, while evils are sufferable, than to right themselves by abolishing the forms to which they are accustomed. But when a long train of abuses and usurpations, pursuing invariably the same object, evinces a design to reduce them under absolute despotism, it is their right, it is their duty, to throw off such government, and to provide new guards for their future security. Such has been the patient sufferance of the colonies, and such is now the necessity which constrains them to alter their former systems of government. The history of the present king of Great Britain is a history of repeated injuries and usurpations, all having in direct object the establishment of an absolute tyranny over these states. To prove this, let facts be submitted to a candid world.

He has refused his assent to laws the most wholesome and necessary for the public good.

He has forbidden his governors to pass laws of immediate and pressing importance, unless suspended in their operations till his assent should be obtained; and, when so suspended, he has utterly neglected to attend to them.

He has refused to pass other laws for the accommodation of large districts of people, unless those people would relinquish the right of representation in the legislature — a right inestimable to them, and formidable to tyrants only.

He has called together legislative bodies a places unusual, uncomfortable, and distant from the repository of their public records, for the sole purpose of fatiguing them into compliance with his measures.

He has dissolved representative houses repeatedly, for opposing, with manly firmness his invasions on the rights of the people.

He has refused, for a long time after such dissolutions, to cause others to be elected; whereby the legislative powers, incapable of annihilation, have returned to the people at large for their exercise; the state remaining, in the mean time, exposed to all the dangers of invasion from without and convulsions within.

He has endeavored to prevent the population

of these states; for that purpose obstructing the laws of naturalization of foreigners, refusing to pass others to encourage their migration thither, and raising the conditions of new appropriations of lands.

He has obstructed the administration of justice, by refusing his assent to laws for establishing judiciary powers.

He has made judges dependent on his will alone, for the tenure of their offices, and the amount and payment of their salaries.

He has erected a multitude of new offices, and sent hither swarms of officers to harass our people, and eat out their substance.

He has kept among us in time of peace, standing armies, without the consent of our legislatures.

He has affected to render the military independent of, and superior to, the civil power.

He has combined with others to subject us to a jurisdiction foreign to our constitution, and unacknowledged by our laws; giving his assent to their acts of pretended legislation,

For quartering large bodies of armed troops among us;

For protecting them, by a mock trial, from

punishment for any murders which they should commit on the inhabitants of these states;

For cutting off our trade with all parts of the world;

For imposing taxes on us without our consent;

For depriving us, in many cases, of the benefit of trial by jury.

For transporting us beyond seas to be tried for pretended offences;

For abolishing the free system of English laws in a neighboring province, establishing therein an arbitrary government, and enlarging its boundaries so as to render it at once an example and fit instrument for introducing the same absolute rule into these colonies;

For taking away our charters, abolishing our most valuable laws, and altering, fundamentally, the forms of our governments;

For suspending our own legislatures, and declaring themselves invested with power to legislate for us in all cases whatsoever.

He has abdicated government here by declaring us out of his protection, and waging war against us.

He has plundered our seas, ravaged our

coasts, burnt our towns, and destroyed the lives of our people.

He is, at this time, transporting large armies of foreign mercenaries to complete the works of death, desolation, and tyranny, with circumstances of cruelty and perfidy scarcely paralleled in the most barbarous ages, and totally unworthy the head of a civilized nation.

He has constrained our fellow-citizens, taken captive on the high seas, to bear arms against their country, to become the executioners of their friends and brethren, or to fall themselves by their hands.

He has excited domestic insurrections amongst us, and has endeavored to bring on the inhabitants of our frontiers the merciless Indian savages, whose known rule of warfare is an undistinguished destruction of all ages, sexes, and conditions.

In every stage of these oppressions, we have petitioned for redress in the most humble terms. Our repeated petitions have been answered only by repeated injury. A prince, whose character is thus marked by every act which may define a tyrant, is unfit to be the ruler of a free people.

Nor have we been wanting in attentions

to our British brethren. We have warned them, from time to time, of the attempts, by their legislature, to extend an unwarrantable jurisdiction over us. We have reminded them of the circumstances of our emigration and settlement here. We have appealed to their native justice and magnanimity, and we have conjured them, by the ties of our common kindred, to disavow these usurpations, which would inevitably interrupt our connections and correspondence. They, too, have been deaf to the voice of justice and of consanguinity. We must, therefore, acquiesce in the necessity which denounces our separation, and hold them, as we hold the rest of mankind, enemies in war, in peace, friends.

We, therefore, the Representatives of the United States of America, in General Congress assembled, appealing to the Supreme Judge of the world for the rectitude of our intentions, do, in the name and by the authority of the good people of these colonies, solemnly publish and declare that these United Colonies are, and of right ought to be, free and independent states, that they are absolved from all allegiance to the British crown, and that all political connection between them and the state of Great Britain is and ought to be, totally dissolved; and that, as free and independent states, they have full power to levy war, conclude peace, contract alliances, establish commerce, and do all other acts and things which independent states may of right do. And, for the support of this declaration, with a firm reliance on the protection of Divine Providence, we mutually pledge to each other our lives, our fortunes, and our sacred honor.

The foregoing declaration was, by order of Congress, engrossed, and signed by the following members:—

JOHN HANCOCK.

New Hampshire.
JOSIAH BARTLETT,
WILLIAM WHIPPLE,
MATTHEW THORNTON.

Massachusetts.
SAMUEL ADAMS,
JOHN ADAMS,
ROBERT TREAT PAINE,
ELBRIDGE GERRY.

Rhode Island.
STEPHEN HOPKINS,
WILLIAM ELLERY.

Connecticut.
ROGER SHERMAN,
SAMUEL HUNTINGTON,
WILLIAM WILLIAMS,

OLIVER WOLCOTT.

New York.
WILLIAM FLOYD,
PHILIP LIVINGSTON,
FRANCIS LEWIS,
LEWIS MORRIS.

New Jersey.
RICHARD STOCKTON,
JOHN WITHERSPOON,
FRANCIS HOPKINSON,
JOHN HART,
ABRAHAM CLARK.

Pennsylvania.
ROBERT MORRIS,
BENJAMIN RUSH,
BENJAMIN FRANKLIN.

JOHN MORTON,
GEORGE CLYMER,
JAMES SMITH,
GEORGE TAYLOR,
JAMES WILSON,
GEORGE ROSS.

Delaware.
CÆSAR RODNEY,
GEORGE READ,
THOMAS M'KEAN.

Maryland.
SAMUEL CHASE,
WILLIAM PACA,
THOMAS STONE,
CHARLES CARROLL, of Carrollton.

Virginia.
GEORGE WYTHE,
RICHARD HENRY LEE,
THOMAS JEFFERSON,
BENJAMIN HARRISON,
THOMAS NELSON, Jr.,
FRANCIS LIGHTFOOT LEE,
CARTER BRAXTON.

North Carolina.
WILLIAM HOOPER,
JOSEPH HEWES,
JOHN PENN.

South Carolina.
EDWARD RUTLEDGE,
THOMAS HEYWARD, Jr.
THOMAS LYNCH, Jr.
ARTHUR MIDDLETON.

Georgia.
BUTTON GWINNETT,
LYMAN HALL,
GEORGE WALTON.

CONSTITUTION OF THE UNITED STATES.

We, the People of the United States, in order to form a more perfect union, establish justice, insure domestic tranquillity, provide for the common defence, promote the general welfare, and secure the blessings of liberty to ourselves and our posterity, do ordain and establish this Constitution for the United States of America.

ARTICLE I.

SECT. I.—All legislative powers herein granted shall be vested in a Congress of the United States, which shall consist of a Senate and House of Representatives.

SECT. II.—1. The House of Representatives shall be composed of members chosen every second year, by the people of the several states; and the electors in each state shall have the qualifications requisite for electors of the most numerous branch of the state legislature.

2. No person shall be a representative who shall not have attained the age of twenty-five years, and been seven years a citizen of the United States, and who shall not, when elected, be an inhabitant of the state in which he shall be chosen.

3. Representatives and direct taxes shall be apportioned among the several states which may be included within this Union, according to their respective numbers, which shall be determined by adding to the whole number of free persons, including those bound to service for a term of years, and excluding Indians not taxed, three fifths of all other persons. The actual enumeration shall be made within three years after the first meeting of the Congress of the United States, and within every subsequent term of ten years, in such manner as they shall by law direct. The number of representatives shall not exceed one for every thirty thousand, but each state shall have at least one representative; and until such enumeration shall be made, the state of *New Hampshire* shall be entitled to choose three; *Massachusetts*, eight, *Rhode Island and Providence Plantations*, one; *Connecticut*, five; *New York*, six; *New Jersey*, four; *Pennsylvania*, eight; *Delaware*, one

Maryland, six; *Virginia*, ten; *North Carolina*, five; *South Carolina*, five; *Georgia*, three.

4. When vacancies happen in the representation from any state, the executive authority thereof shall issue writs of election to fill such vacancies.

5. The House of Representatives shall choose their speaker and other officers, and shall have the sole power of impeachment.

SECT. III.—1. The Senate of the United States shall be composed of two senators from each state, chosen by the legislature thereof, for six years; and each senator shall have one vote.

2. Immediately after they shall be assembled in consequence of the first election, they shall be divided, as equally as may be, into three classes. The seats of the senators of the first class shall be vacated at the expiration of the second year, of the second class at the expiration of the fourth year, and the third class at the expiration of the sixth year, so that one third may be chosen every second year; and if vacancies happen by resignation or otherwise, during the recess of the legislature of any state, the executive thereof may make temporary appointments until the next meeting of the

legislature, which shall then fill such vacancies.

3. No person shall be a senator who shall not have attained the age of thirty years, and been nine years a citizen of the United States, and who shall not, when elected, be an inhabitant of that state for which he shall be chosen.

4. The Vice-President of the United States shall be President of the Senate, but shall have no vote unless they be equally divided.

5. The Senate shall choose their other officers, and also a president pro tempore in the absence of the Vice-President, or when he shall exercise the office of President of the United States.

6. The Senate shall have the sole power to try all impeachments. When sitting for that purpose, they shall be on oath or affirmation. When the President of the United States is tried, the Chief Justice shall preside; and no person shall be convicted without the concurrence of two thirds of the members present.

7. Judgment, in cases of impeachment, shall not extend further than to removal from office, and disqualification to hold and enjoy any office of honor, trust, or profit under the United States; but the party convicted shall, neverthe-

.ess, be liable and subject to indictment, trial, judgment and punishment according to law.

Sect. IV.—1. The times, places, and manner of holding elections for senators and representatives shall be prescribed in each state by the legislature thereof; but the Congress may, at any time, by law, make or alter such regulations, except as to the places of choosing senators.

2. The Congress shall assemble at least once in every year: and such meeting shall be on the first Monday in December, unless they shall by law appoint a different day.

Sect. V.—1. Each house shall be judge of the elections, returns, and qualifications of its own members; and a majority of each shall constitute a quorum to do business; but a smaller number may adjourn from day to day, and may be authorized to compel the attendance of absent members, in such manner, and under such penalties, as each house may provide.

2. Each house may determine the rules of its proceedings, punish its members for disorderly behavior, and, with the concurrence of two thirds, expel a member.

3. Each house shall keep a journal of its

proceedings, and from time to time publish the same, excepting such parts as may, in their judgment, require secrecy; and the yeas and nays of the members of either house on any question shall, at the desire of one fifth of those present, be entered on the journal.

4. Neither house, during the session of Congress, shall, without the consent of the other, adjourn for more than three days, nor to any other place than that in which the two houses shall be sitting.

Sect. VI.—1. The senators and representatives shall receive a compensation for their services, to be ascertained by law, and paid out of the treasury of the United States. They shall, in all cases, except treason, felony, and breach of the peace, be privileged from arrest, during their attendance at the session of their respective houses, and in going to, or returning from the same; and for any speech or debate in either house, they shall not be questioned in any other place.

2. No senator or representative shall, during the time for which he was elected, be appointed to any civil office under the authority of the United States, which shall have been created or the emoluments whereof shall have been in-

creased, during such time; and no person holding any office under the United States shall be a member of either house, during his continuance in office.

Sect. VII.—1. All bills for raising revenue shall originate in the House of Representatives; but the Senate may propose or concur with amendments, as on other bills.

2. Every bill, which shall have passed the House of Representatives and the Senate, shall, before it become a law, be presented to the President of the United States; if he approve, he shall sign it; but if not, he shall return it, with his objections, to that house in which it shall have originated, who shall enter the objections at large on their journal, and proceed to reconsider it. If, after such reconsideration, two thirds of that house shall agree to pass the bill, it shall be sent, together with the objections, to the other house, and if approved by two thirds of that house, it shall become a law. But in all such cases, the votes of both houses shall be determined by yeas and nays; and the names of the persons voting for and against the bill shall be entered on the journals of each house respectively. If any bill shall not be returned by the President within ten days

(Sundays excepted) after it shall have been presented to him, the same shall be a law, in like manner as if he had signed it, unless Congress, by their adjournment, prevent its return; in which case it shall not be a law.

3. Every order, resolution, or vote to which the concurrence of the Senate and House of Representatives may be necessary, (except on a question of adjournment,) shall be presented to the President of the United States; and before the same shall take effect, shall be approved by him, or being disapproved by him, shall be repassed by two thirds of the Senate and House of Representatives, according to the rules and limitations prescribed in the case of a bill.

Sect. VIII. — The Congress shall have power —

1. To lay and collect taxes, duties, imposts, and excises; to pay the debts and provide for the common defence and general welfare of the United States; but all duties, imposts and excises shall be uniform throughout the United States:

2. To borrow money on the credit of the United States:

3. To regulate commerce with foreign na-

tions and among the several states, and with Indian tribes:

4. To establish a uniform rule of naturalization, and uniform laws on the subject of bankruptcies, throughout the United States:

5. To coin money, regulate the value thereof and of foreign coin, and fix the standard of weights and measures:

6. To provide for the punishment of counterfeiting the securities and current coin of the United States:

7. To establish post offices and post roads:

8. To promote the progress of science and useful arts, by securing for limited times, to authors and inventors, the exclusive right to their respective writings and discoveries:

9. To constitute tribunals inferior to the supreme court:

10. To define and punish piracies and felonies committed on the high seas, and offences against the law of nations:

11. To declare war, grant letters of marque and reprisal, and make rules concerning captures on land and water:

12. To raise and support armies; but no appropriation of money to that use shall be for a longer term than two years:

13. To provide and maintain a navy:

14. To make rules for the government and regulation of the land and naval forces:

15. To provide for calling forth the militia to execute the laws of the Union, suppress insurrections, and repel invasions:

16. To provide for organizing, arming, and disciplining the militia, and for governing such part of them as may be employed in the service of the United States, reserving to the states respectively the appointment of the officers, and the authority of training the militia, according to the discipline prescribed by Congress:

17. To exercise exclusive legislation, in all cases whatsoever, over such district (not exceeding ten miles square) as may, by cession of particular states, and the acceptance of Congress, become the seat of government of the United States, and to exercise like authority over all places purchased by the consent of the legislature of the state in which the same shall be, for the erection of forts, magazines, arsenals, dockyards, and other needful buildings: And,

18. To make all laws which shall be necessary and proper for carrying into execution the foregoing powers, and all other powers vested by this constitution in the government of the

United States, or in any department or officer thereof.

Sect. IX.—1. The migration or importation of such persons as any of the states now existing shall think proper to admit, shall not be prohibited by the Congress prior to the year one thousand eight hundred and eight; but a tax or duty may be imposed on such importation, not exceeding ten dollars for each person.

2. The privilege of the writ of habeas corpus shall not be suspended, unless when, in cases of rebellion or invasion, the public safety may require it.

3. No bill of attainder, or ex post facto law, shall be passed.

4. No capitation or other direct tax shall be laid, unless in proportion to the census or enumeration herein before directed to be taken.

5. No tax or duty shall be laid on articles exported from any state. No preference shall be given, by any regulation of commerce or revenue, to the ports of one state over those of another; nor shall vessels bound to or from one state be obliged to enter, clear, or pay duties in another.

6. No money shall be drawn from the trea-

sury, but in consequence of appropriations made by law; and a regular statement and account of the receipts and expenditures of all public money shall be published from time to time.

7. No title of nobility shall be granted by the United States; and no person holding any office of profit or trust under them, shall, without the consent of the Congress, accept of any present, emolument, office, or title of any kind whatever, from any king, prince or foreign state.

Sect. X.—1. No state shall enter into any treaty, alliance, or confederation; grant letters of marque and reprisal; coin money; emit bills of credit; make anything but gold and silver coin a tender in payment of debts; pass any bill of attainder, ex post facto law, or law impairing the obligation of contracts; or grant any title of nobility.

2. No state shall, without the consent of Congress, lay any imposts or duties on imports or exports, except what may be absolutely necessary for executing its inspection laws; and the net produce of all duties and imposts laid by any state on imports or exports, shall be for the use of the treasury of the United States; and all such laws shall be subject to the revision

and control of the Congress. No state shall, without the consent of Congress, lay any duty on tonnage, keep troops or ships of war in time of peace, enter into any agreement or compact with another state or with a foreign power, or engage in war, unless actually invaded, or in such imminent danger as will not admit of delay.

ARTICLE II.

Sect. I.—1. The executive power shall be vested in a President of the United States of America. He shall hold his office during the term of four years, and, together with the Vice-President, chosen for the same term, be elected as follows:

2. Each state shall appoint, in such manner as the legislature thereof may direct, a number of electors, equal to the whole number of senators and representatives to which the state may be entitled in the Congress; but no senator or representative, or person holding an office of trust or profit under the United States, shall be appointed an elector.

3. [Annulled. See Amendments, art. 12.]

4. The Congress may determine the time of choosing the electors, and the day on which

they shall give their votes; which day shall be the same throughout the United States.

5. No person, except a natural-born citizen, or a citizen of the United States at the time of the adoption of this constitution, shall be eligible to the office of President; neither shall any person be eligible to that office, who shall not have attained the age of thirty-five years, and been fourteen years a resident within the United States.

6. In case of the removal of the President from office, or of his death, resignation, or inability to discharge the powers and duties of said office, the same shall devolve on the Vice-President; and the Congress may by law provide for the case of removal, death, resignation, or inability, both of the President and Vice-President, declaring what officer shall then act as President, and such officer shall act accordingly, until the disability be removed, or a President shall be elected.

7. The President shall, at stated times, receive for his services a compensation which shall neither be increased nor diminished during the period for which he shall have been elected; and he shall not receive within that period,

any other emolument from the United States, or any of them.

8. Before he enter on the execution of his office, he shall take the following oath or affirmation:—

"I do solemnly swear, (or affirm) that I will faithfully execute the office of President of the United States, and will, to the best of my ability, preserve, protect and defend the constitution of the United States."

Sect. II.—1. The President shall be commander-in-chief of the army and navy of the United States, and of the militia of the several states, when called into the actual service of the United States: he may require the opinion, in writing, of the principal officer in each of the executive departments, upon any subject relating to the duties of their respective offices; and he shall have power to grant reprieves and pardons for offences against the United States, except in cases of impeachment.

2. He shall have power, by and with the advice and consent of the Senate, to make treaties, provided two thirds of the senators present concur; and he shall nominate, and by and with the advice and consent of the Senate, shall appoint ambassadors, other public ministers and consuls

judges of the supreme court, and all other officers of the United States, whose appointments are not herein otherwise provided for, and which shall be established by law. But the Congress may, by law, vest the appointment of such inferior officers as they think proper in the President alone, in the courts of law, or in the heads of departments.

3. The President shall have power to fill up all vacancies that may happen during the recess of the Senate, by granting commissions, which shall expire at the end of their next session.

Sect. III.—He shall, from time to time, give to the Congress information of the state of the Union, and recommend to their consideration such measures as he shall judge necessary and expedient; he may, on extraordinary occasions, convene both houses, or either of them, and in case of disagreement between them with respect to the time of adjournment, he may adjourn them to such time as he shall think proper; he shall receive ambassadors, and other public ministers; he shall take care that the laws be faithfully executed; and shall commission all the officers of the United States.

Sect. IV.—The President, Vice-President

and all civil officers of the United States, shall be removed from office on impeachment for, and conviction of, treason, bribery, or other high crimes and misdemeanors.

ARTICLE III.

SECT. I.—The judicial power of the United States shall be vested in one supreme court, and in such inferior courts as the Congress may, from time to time, ordain and establish. The judges, both of the supreme and inferior courts, shall hold their offices during good behavior, and shall, at stated times, receive for their services a compensation which shall not be diminished during their continuance in office.

SECT. II.—1. The judicial power shall extend to all cases in law and equity arising under this constitution, the laws of the United States, and treaties made, or which shall be made, under their authority; to all cases affecting ambassadors, and other public ministers and consuls; to all cases of admiralty and maritime jurisdiction; to controversies to which the United States shall be a party; to controversies between two or more states; between a state and citizens of another state; between citizens of different states; between citizens of the same state claiming lands under grants of different states, and between a state, or the citizens thereof, and foreign states, citizens, or subjects.

2. In all cases affecting ambassadors, other public ministers and consuls, and those in which a state shall be a party, the supreme court shall have original jurisdiction. In all other cases before mentioned, the supreme court shall have appellate jurisdiction, both as to law and fact, with such exceptions, and under such regulations, as the Congress shall make.

3. The trial of all crimes, except in cases of impeachment, shall be by jury; and such trial shall be held in the state where the said crimes shall have been committed; but when not committed within any state, the trial shall be at such a place or places as the Congress may by law have directed.

Sect. III.—1. Treason against the United States shall consist only in levying war against them, or in adhering to their enemies, giving them aid and comfort. No person shall be convicted of treason, unless on the testimony of two witnesses to the same overt act, or confessions in open court.

2. The Congress shall have power to declare the punishment of treason; but no attain-

der of treason shall work corruption of blood, or forfeiture, except during the life of the person attainted.

ARTICLE IV.

Sect. I.—Full faith and credit shall be given in each state to the public acts, records, and judicial proceedings of every other state. And the Congress may, by general laws, prescribe the manner in which such acts, records, and proceedings shall be proved, and the effect thereof.

Sect. II.—1. The citizens of each state shall be entitled to all privileges and immunities of citizens in the several states.

2. A person charged in any state with treason, felony, or other crime, who shall flee from justice, and be found in another state, shall, on demand of the executive authority of the state from which he fled, be delivered up to be removed to the state having jurisdiction of the crime.

3. No person held to service or labor in one state, under the laws thereof, escaping into another, shall, in consequence of any law or regulation therein, be discharged from such service or labor, but shall be delivered up on

claim of the party to whom such service or labor may be due.

Sect. III.—1. New states may be admitted by the Congress into this Union; but no new state shall be formed or erected within the jurisdiction of any other state; nor any state be formed by the junction of two or more states, or parts of states, without the consent of the legislature of the states concerned, as well as of the Congress.

2. The Congress shall have power to dispose of and make all needful rules and regulations respecting the territory or other property belonging to the United States; and nothing in this constitution shall be so construed as to prejudice any claims of the United States, or of any particular state.

Sect. IV.—The United States shall guaranty to every state of this Union a republican form of government, and shall protect each of them against invasion, and, on application of the legislature, or of the executive, (when the legislature cannot be convened,) against domestic violence.

ARTICLE V.

The Congress, whenever two thirds of both houses shall deem it necessary, shall propose amendments to this constitution, or, on the application of the legislature of two thirds of the several states, shall call a convention for proposing amendments, which, in either case, shall be valid to all intents and purposes, as part of this constitution, when ratified by the legislatures of three fourths of the several states, or by conventions in three fourths thereof, as the one or the other mode of ratification may be proposed by the Congress; provided that no amendment which may be made prior to the year one thousand eight hundred and eight, shall in any manner affect the first and fourth clauses in the ninth section of the first article; and that no state, without its consent, shall be deprived of its equal suffrage in the Senate.

ARTICLE VI.

1. All debts contracted, and engagements entered into, before the adoption of this constitution, shall be as valid against the United States under this constitution, as under the confederation.

2. This constitution, and the laws of the United States which shall be made in pursuance thereof, and all treaties made, or which shall be made, under the authority of the United

States, shall be the supreme law of the land; and the judges in every state shall be bound thereby; anything in the constitution or laws of any state to the contrary notwithstanding.

3. The senators and representatives before mentioned, and the members of the several state legislatures, and all the executive and judicial officers, both of the United States and of the several states, shall be bound by oath or affirmation to support this constitution; but no religious test shall ever be required as a qualification to any office or public trust under the United States.

ARTICLE VII.

The ratification of the conventions of nine states shall be sufficient for the establishment of this constitution between the states so ratifying the same.

Done in convention, by the unanimous consent of the states present, the seventeenth day of September, in the year of our Lord one thousand seven hundred and eighty-seven, and of the Independence of the United States of America the twelfth. In witness whereof, we have hereunto subscribed our names.

CONSTITUTION.

GEORGE WASHINGTON,

President and Deputy from Virginia.

New Hampshire.
JOHN LANGDON,
NICHOLAS GILMAN.

Massachusetts.
NATHANIEL GORHAM,
RUFUS KING.

Connecticut.
WM. SAMUEL JOHNSON,
ROGER SHERMAN.

New York.
ALEXANDER HAMILTON.

New Jersey.
WILLIAM LIVINGSTON,
DAVID BREARLY,
WILLIAM PATTERSON,
JONATHAN DAYTON.

Pennsylvania.
BENJAMIN FRANKLIN,
THOMAS MIFFLIN,
ROBERT MORRIS,
GEORGE CLYMER,
THOMAS FITZSIMONS,
JARED INGERSOLL,
JAMES WILSON,
GOUVERNEUR MORRIS.

Delaware.
GEORGE READ,
GUNNING BEDFORD, JR
JOHN DICKERSON,
RICHARD BASSET,
JACOB BROOM.

Maryland.
JAMES M'HENRY,
DAN' of ST. T. JENIFER,
DANIEL CARROLL.

Virginia.
JOHN BLAIR,
JAMES MADISON, JR.

North Carolina.
WILLIAM BLOUNT,
RICH. DOBBS SPAIGHT,
HUGH WILLIAMSON.

South Carolina.
JOHN RUTLEDGE,
CHARLES C. PINCKNEY,
CHARLES PINCKNEY,
PIERCE BUTLER.

Georgia.
WILLIAM FEW,
ABRAHAM BALDWIN.

Attest,   WILLIAM JACKSON, *Secretary.*

AMENDMENTS TO THE CONSTITUTION.

Art. I.—Congress shall make no law respecting an establishment of religion, or prohibiting the free exercise thereof; or abridging the freedom of speech, or of the press; or the right of the people peaceably to assemble and to petition the government for a redress of grievances.

Art. II.—A well-regulated militia being necessary for the security of a free state, the right of the people to keep and bear arms shall not be infringed.

Art. III.—No soldier shall, in time of peace, be quartered in any house without the consent of the owner, nor in time of war, but in a manner to be prescribed by law.

Art. IV.—The right of the people to be secure in their persons, houses, papers, and effects, against unreasonable searches and seizures, shall not be violated; and no warrants shall issue but upon probable cause, supported by oath or affirmation, and particularly describing the place to be searched, and the persons or things to be seized.

Art. V.—No person shall be held to answer for a capital, or otherwise infamous crime, unless on a presentment or indictment of a grand jury, except in cases arising in the land or naval forces, or in the militia when in actual service, in time of war or public danger; nor shall any person be subject for the same offence to be twice put in jeopardy of life or limb; nor shall be compelled, in any criminal case, to be witness against himself, nor be deprived of life, liberty, or property, without due process of law; nor shall private property be taken for public use without just compensation.

Art. VI.—In all criminal prosecutions, the accused shall enjoy the right to a speedy and public trial, by an impartial jury of the state and district wherein the crime shall have been committed, which district shall have been previously ascertained by law, and to be informed of the nature and cause of the accusation; to be confronted with the witnesses against him; to have compulsory process for obtaining witnesses in his favor; and to have the assistance of counsel for his defence.

Art. VII.—In suits of common law, where the value in controversy shall exceed twenty dollars, the right of trial by jury shall be preserved; and no fact tried by a jury shall be otherwise reëxamined in any court of the United States than according to the rules of the common law.

Art. VIII.—Excessive bail shall not be required, nor excessive fines imposed, nor cruel and unusual punishments inflicted.

Art. IX.—The enumeration, in the constitution, of certain rights, shall not be construed to deny or disparage others retained by the people.

Art. X.—The powers not delegated to the United States by the constitution, nor prohibited by it to the states, are reserved to the states respectively, or to the people.

Art. XI.—The judicial power of the United States shall not be construed to extend to any suit in law or equity commenced or prosecuted against one of the United States by citizens of another state, or by citizens or subjects of any foreign state.

Art. XII.—The electors shall meet in their respective states, and vote by ballot for President and Vice-President, one of whom, at least, shall not be an inhabitant of the same state with themselves, they shall name in their ballots the person voted for as President, and in distinct ballots the person voted for as Vice-President; and they shall make distinct lists of all persons voted for as President, and of all persons voted for as Vice-President, and of the number of votes for each; which lists they shall sign and certify, and transmit sealed to the seat of government of the United States, directed to the President of the Senate. The President of the Senate shall, in the presence of the Senate and House of Representatives, open all the certificates, and the votes shall then be counted; the person having the greatest number of votes for President, shall be President, if such number be a majority of the whole number of electors appointed; and if no person have such majority, then, from the persons having the highest number, not exceeding three, on the list of those voted for as President, the House of Representatives shall choose immediately, by ballot, the President. But, in choosing the President, the votes shall be taken by states, the representation from each state having one vote; a quorum for this purpose shall consist of a member or members from two thirds of the states, and a majority of all the states shall be necessary to a choice. And if the House of Representatives shall not choose a President, whenever the right of choice shall devolve upon them, before the fourth day of March next following, then the Vice-President shall act as President, as in the case of the death or other constitutional disability of the President.

2. The person having the greatest number of votes as Vice-President shall be the Vice-President, if such number be a majority of the whole number of electors appointed; and if no person have a majority, then, from the two highest numbers on the list, the Senate shall choose the Vice-President; a quorum for the purpose shall consist of two thirds of the whole number of senators, and a majority of the whole number shall be necessary to a choice.

3. But no person constitutionally ineligible to the office of President, shall be eligible to that of Vice-President of the United States.

ART. XIII.—If any citizen of the United States shall accept, claim, receive, or retain any title of nobility or honor, or shall, without the consent of Congress, accept or retain any present, pension, office or emolument of any kind whatever, from any emperor, king, prince, or foreign power, such person shall cease to be a citizen of the United States, and shall be incapable of holding any office of trust or profit under them or either of them.

WASHINGTON'S INAUGURAL ADDRESS.

April 30, 1789.

*Fellow-Citizens of the Senate
and House of Representatives:*

AMONG the vicissitudes incident to life, no event could have filled me with greater anxieties than that of which the notification was transmitted by your order, and received on the 14th day of the present month. On the one hand, I was summoned by my country, whose voice I can never hear but with veneration and love, from a retreat which I had chosen with the fondest predilection, and, in my flattering hopes, with an immutable decision, as the asylum of my declining years, a retreat which was rendered every day more necessary as well as more dear to me by the addition of habit to inclination, and of frequent interruptions in my health, to the gradual waste committed on it by time. On the other hand, the magnitude and difficulty of the trust to which the voice of my country called me, being sufficient to awaken in the wisest and most experienced of her citizens a distrustful scrutiny into his qualifications, could not but overwhelm with despondency one who, inheriting inferior endowments from nature, and unpractised in the duties of civil administration, ought to be peculiarly conscious of his own deficiencies. In this conflict of emotions, all that I dare aver is, that it has been my faithful study to collect my duty from a just appreciation of every circumstance by which it might be affected. All I dare hope is, that if, in executing this task, I have been too much swayed by a grateful remembrance of former instances, or by an affectionate sensibility to this transcendent proof of the confidence of my fellow-citizens, and have thence too little consulted my incapacity as well as disinclination for the weighty and untried cares before me, my error will be palliated by the motives which misled me, and its consequences be judged by my country with some share of the partiality with which they originated.

Such being the impressions under which I have, in obedience to the public summons, repaired to the present station, it would be peculiarly improper to omit, in this first official act, my fervent supplications to that Almighty Being who rules over the universe, who presides in the councils of nations, and whose providential aids can supply every human defect, that his benediction may consecrate to the liberties and happiness of the people of the United States a government instituted by themselves for these essential purposes, and may enable every instrument employed in its administration to execute with success the functions allotted to his charge. In tendering this homage to the great Author of every public and private good, I assure myself that it expresses your sentiments not less than my own, nor those of my fellow-citizens at large less than either. No people can be bound to acknowledge and adore the invisible hand which conducts the affairs of men, more than the people of the United States. Every step by which they have advanced to the character of an independent nation seems to have been distinguished by some token of providential agency; and in the important revolution just accomplished in the system of their united government, the tranquil deliberations and voluntary consent of so many distinct communities, from which the event has resulted, cannot be compared with the means by which most governments have been established without some return of pious gratitude, along with an humble anticipation of the future blessings which the past seems to presage. These reflections, arising out of the present crisis, have forced themselves too strongly on my mind to be suppressed. You will join with me, I trust, in thinking that there are none under the influence of which the proceedings of a new and free government can more auspiciously commence.

By the article establishing the executive department, it is made the duty of the President "to recommend to your consideration such measures as he shall judge necessary and expedient." The circumstances under which I now meet you will acquit me from entering into that subject further than to refer to the great constitutional charter under which you are assembled, and which, in defining your powers, designates the objects to which your attention is to be given. It will be more consistent with those circumstances, and far more congenial with the feelings which actuate me, to substitute, in place of a recommendation of particular measures, the tribute that is due to

the talents, the rectitude, and the patriotism
which adorn the characters selected to devise
and adopt them. In these honorable qualifications I behold the surest pledges that as, on one
side, no local prejudices or attachments, no
separate views nor party animosities, will misdirect the comprehensive and equal eye which
ought to watch over this great assemblage of
communities and interests, so, on another, that
the foundations of our national policy will be
laid in the pure and immutable principles of
private morality; and the preëminence of free
government be exemplified by all the attributes
which can win the affections of its citizens, and
command the respect of the world. I dwell on
this prospect with every satisfaction which an
ardent love for my country can inspire, since
there is no truth more thoroughly established
than that there exists in the economy and
course of nature an indissoluble union between
virtue and happiness; between duty and advantage; between the genuine maxims of an honest and magnanimous policy and the solid
rewards of public prosperity and felicity; since
we ought to be less persuaded that the propitious smiles of Heaven can never be expected
on a nation that disregards the eternal rules of

order and right which Heaven itself has ordained, and since the preservation of the sacred fire of liberty, and the destiny of the republican model of government, are justly considered as deeply, perhaps as finally, staked on the experiment intrusted to the hands of the American people.

Besides the ordinary objects submitted to your care, it will remain with your judgment to decide how far an exercise of the occasional power delegated by the fifth article of the constitution is rendered expedient, at the present juncture, by the nature of the objections which have been urged against the system, or by the degree of inquietude which has given birth to them. Instead of undertaking particular recommendations on this subject, in which I could be guided by no lights derived from official opportunities, I shall again give way to my entire confidence in your discernment and pursuit of the public good; for I assure myself that while you carefully avoid every alteration which might endanger the benefits of a united and effective government, or which ought to await the future lessons of experience, a reverence for the characteristic rights of freemen, and a regard for the public harmony, will sufficiently influence your deliberations on the question how far the former can be more impregnably fortified, or the latter be safely and advantageously promoted.

To the preceding observations I have one to add, which will be most properly addressed to the House of Representatives. It concerns myself, and will therefore be as brief as possible. When I was first honored with a call into the service of my country, then on the eve of an arduous struggle for its liberties, the light in which I contemplated my duty required that I should renounce every pecuniary compensation. From this resolution I have in no instance departed; and being still under the impressions which produced it, I must decline, as inapplicable to myself, any share in the personal emoluments which may be indispensably included in a permanent provision for the executive department, and must accordingly pray that the pecuniary estimates for the station in which I am placed, may, during my continuance in it, be limited to such actual expenditures as the public good may be thought to require.

Having thus imparted to you my sentiments as they have been awakened by the occasion which brings us together, I shall take my present leave, but not without resorting once more to the benign Parent of the human race, in humble supplication that, since he has been pleased to favor the American people with opportunities for deliberating in perfect tranquillity, and dispositions for deciding with unparalleled unanimity on a form of government for the security of their union and the advancement of their happiness, so his divine blessing may be equally conspicuous in the enlarged views, the temperate consultations, and the wise measures on which the success of this government must depend.

WASHINGTON'S FIRST ANNUAL ADDRESS.
January 8, 1790.

*Fellow-Citizens of the Senate
and House of Representatives:*

I EMBRACE with great satisfaction the opportunity which now presents itself of congratulating you on the present favorable prospects of our public affairs. The recent accession of the important state of North Carolina to the constitution of the United States, (of which official information has been received,) the rising credit and respectability of our country, the general and increasing good-will towards the government of the Union, and the concord, peace and plenty, with which we are blessed, are circumstances auspicious, in an eminent degree, to our national prosperity.

In resuming your consultations for the general good, you cannot but derive encouragement from the reflection that the measures of the last session have been as satisfactory to your constituents as the novelty and difficulty of the work allowed you to hope. Still further to realize their expectations, and to secure the blessings which a gracious Providence has placed within our reach, will, in the course of the present important session, call for the cool and deliberate exertion of your patriotism, firmness, and wisdom.

Among the many interesting objects which will engage your attention, that of providing for the common defence will merit particular regard. To be prepared for war, is one of the most effectual means of preserving peace.

A free people ought not only to be armed, but disciplined; to which end a uniform and well-digested plan is requisite: and their safety and interest require that they should promote such manufactures as tend to render them independent of others for essential, particularly military supplies.

The proper establishment of the troops which may be deemed indispensable will be entitled to mature consideration. In the arrangements which may be made respecting it, it will be of importance to conciliate the comfortable support of the officers and soldiers, with a due regard to economy.

There was reason to hope that the pacific measures, adopted with regard to certain hostile tribes of Indians, would have relieved the inhabitants of our southern and western frontiers from their depredations; but you will perceive, from the information contained in the papers which I shall direct to be laid before you, (comprehending a communication from the Commonwealth of Virginia,) that we ought to be prepared to afford protection to those parts of the Union, and, if necessary, to punish aggressors.

The interests of the United States require that our intercourse with other nations should be facilitated by such provisions as will enable me to fulfil my duty in that respect in the manner which circumstances may render most conducive to the public good, and, to this end, that the compensations to be made to the persons who may be employed should, according to the nature of their appointments, be defined by law; and a competent fund designated for defraying the expenses incident to the conduct of our foreign affairs

Various considerations also render it expedient that the terms on which foreigners may be admitted to the rights of citizens should be speedily ascertained by a uniform rule of naturalization.

Uniformity in the currency, weights, and measures of the United States, is an object of great importance, and will, I am persuaded, be duly attended to.

The advancement of agriculture, commerce, and manufactures, by all proper means, will not, I trust, need recommendation; but I cannot forbear intimating to you the expediency of giving effectual encouragement, as well to the introduction of new and useful inventions from abroad, as to the exertions of skill and genius in producing them at home; and of facilitating the intercourse between the distant parts of our country by a due attention to the post-office and post-roads.

Nor am I less persuaded that you will agree with me in opinion, that there is nothing which can better deserve your patronage than the promotion of science and literature. Knowledge is in every country the surest basis of public happiness. In one in which the measures of government receive their impressions so immediately from the sense of the community as in ours, it is proportionably essential. To the security of a free constitution it contributes in various ways; by convincing those who are entrusted with the public administration that every valuable end of government is best answered by the enlightened confidence of the people; and by teaching the people themselves to know and to value their own rights; to discern and provide against invasions of them; to distinguish between oppression and the necessary exercise of lawful authority; between burdens proceeding from a disregard to their convenience, and those resulting from the inevitable exigencies of society; to discriminate the spirit of liberty from that of licentiousness, cherishing the first, avoiding the last, and uniting a speedy but temperate vigilance against encroachments, with an inviolable respect to the laws.

Whether this desirable object will be best promoted by affording aids to seminaries of learning already established, by the institution of a national university, or by any other expedients, will be well worthy of a place in the deliberations of the legislature.

Gentlemen of the House of Representatives:

I saw with peculiar pleasure, at the close of the last session, the resolution entered into by you, expressive of your opinion that an adequate provision for the support of the public credit is a matter of high importance to the national honor and prosperity. In this sentiment I entirely concur. And, to a perfect confidence in your best endeavours to devise such a provision as will be truly consistent with the end, I add an equal reliance on the cheerful coöperation of the other branch of the legislature. It would be superfluous to specify inducements to a measure in which the character and permanent interest of the United States are so obviously and so deeply concerned, and which has received so explicit a sanction from your declaration.

Gentlemen of the Senate
   and House of Representatives:

I have directed the proper officers to lay before you, respectively, such papers and estimates as regard the affairs particularly recommended to your consideration, and necessary to convey to you that information of the state of the Union which it is my duty to afford.

The welfare of our country is the great object to which our cares and efforts ought to be directed. And I shall derive great satisfaction from a coöperation with you in the pleasing though arduous task of insuring to our fellow-citizens the blessings which they have a right to expect from a free, efficient, and equal government.

WASHINGTON'S FAREWELL ADDRESS.

September 17, 1796.

Friends and Fellow-Citizens:

The period for a new election of a citizen to administer the executive government of the United States being not far distant, and the time actually arrived when your thoughts must be employed in designating the person who is to be clothed with that important trust, it appears to me proper, especially as it may conduce to a more distinct expression of the public voice, that I should now apprize you of the resolution I have formed, to decline being considered among the number of those out of whom the choice is to be made.

I beg you, at the same time, to do me the justice to be assured, that this resolution has not been taken without a strict regard to all the considerations appertaining to the relation which binds a dutiful citizen to his country;

and that, in withdrawing the tender of service, which silence in my situation might imply, I am influenced by no diminution of zeal for your future interest; no deficiency of grateful respect for your past kindness; but am supported by a full conviction that the step is compatible with both.

The acceptance of, and continuance hitherto in, the office to which your suffrages have twice called me, have been a uniform sacrifice of inclination to the opinion of duty, and to a deference for what appeared to be your desire. I constantly hoped that it would have been much earlier in my power, consistently with motives which I was not at liberty to disregard, to return to that retirement from which I had been reluctantly drawn. The strength of my inclination to do this, previous to the last election, had even led to the preparation of an address to declare it to you; but mature reflection on the then perplexed and critical posture of affairs with foreign nations, and the unanimous advice of persons entitled to my confidence, impelled me to abandon the idea. I rejoice that the state of your concerns, external as well as internal, no longer renders the pursuit of inclination incompatible with the sentiment of duty or propriety; and am persuaded, whatever partiality may be retained for my services, that, in the present circumstances of our country, you will not disapprove of my determination to retire.

The impressions with which I first undertook the arduous trust were explained on the proper occasion. In the discharge of this trust, I will only say, that I have, with good intentions, contributed towards the organization and administration of the government the best exertions of which a very fallible judgment was capable. Not unconscious, in the outset, of the inferiority of my qualifications, experience, in my own eyes, perhaps still more in the eyes of others, has strengthened the motives to diffidence of myself; and, every day, the increasing weight of years admonishes me more and more, that the shade of retirement is as necessary to me as it will be welcome. Satisfied that if any circumstances have given peculiar value to my services, they were temporary, I have the consolation to believe that while choice and prudence invite me to quit the political scene, patriotism does not forbid it.

In looking forward to the moment which is to terminate the career of my political life, my feelings do not permit me to suspend the deep acknowledgment of that debt of gratitude which I owe to my beloved country for the many honors it has conferred upon me; still more for the steadfast confidence with which it has supported me; and for the opportunities I have thence enjoyed of manifesting my inviolable attachment, by services faithful and persevering, though in usefulness unequal to my zeal. If benefits have resulted to our country from these services, let it always be remembered to your praise, and as an instructive example in our annals, that under circumstances in which the passions, agitated in every direction, were liable to mislead, amidst appearances sometimes dubious, vicissitudes of fortune often discouraging, in situations in which not unfrequently want of success has countenanced the spirit of criticism, the constancy of your support was the essential prop of the efforts, and a guaranty of the plans, by which they were effected. Profoundly penetrated with this idea, I shall carry it with me to the grave, as a strong incitement to unceasing wishes that Heaven may continue to you the choicest tokens of its beneficence—that your union and brotherly affection may be perpetual—that the free constitution which is the work of your hands may be sacredly maintained—that its administration in every department may be stamped with wisdom and virtue—that, in fine, the happiness of the people of these states, under the auspices of liberty, may be made complete, by so careful a preservation and so prudent a use of this blessing, as will acquire to them the glory of recommending it to the applause, the affection, and adoption of every nation which is yet a stranger to it.

Here, perhaps, I ought to stop. But a solicitude for your welfare, which cannot end but with my life, and the apprehension of danger, natural to that solicitude, urge me, on an occasion like the present, to offer to your solemn contemplation, and to recommend to your frequent review, some sentiments, which are the result of much reflection, of no inconsiderable observation, and which appear to me all-important to the permanency of your felicity as a people. These will be offered to you with the more freedom, as you can only see in them the disinterested warnings of a parting friend, who can possibly have no personal motives to bias his counsel. Nor can I forget, as an encouragement to it, your indulgent reception of my sentiments on a former and not dissimilar occasion.

Interwoven as is the love of liberty with every ligament of our hearts, no recommendation of mine is necessary to fortify or confirm the attachment.

The unity of government, which constitutes you one people, is also now dear to you. It is justly so; for it is a main pillar in the edifice of your real independence; the support of your tranquillity at home; your peace abroad; of your safety; of your prosperity; of that very liberty which you so highly prize. But as it is easy to foresee, that, from different causes and from different quarters, much pains will be taken, many artifices employed, to weaken in your minds the conviction of this truth; as this is the point in your political fortress against which the batteries of internal and external enemies will be most constantly and actively (though often covertly and insidiously) directed; it is of infinite moment, that you should properly estimate the immense value of your national union to your collective and individual happiness; that you should cherish a cordial, habitual, and immovable attachment to it; accustoming yourselves to think and to speak of it as a palladium of your political safety and prosperity; watching for its preservation with jealous anxiety; discountenancing whatever may suggest even a suspicion that it can in any event be abandoned; and indignantly frowning upon the first dawning of every attempt to alienate any portion of our country from the rest, or to enfeeble the sacred ties which now link together the various parts.

For this you have every inducement of sympathy and interest. Citizens, by birth or choice, of a common country, that country has a right to concentrate your affections. The name of AMERICAN, which belongs to you in your national capacity, must always exalt the just pride of patriotism more than any appellation derived from local discriminations. With slight shades of difference, you have the same religion, manners, habits, and political principle. You have, in a common cause, fought and triumphed together; the independence and liberty you possess are the work of joint councils and joint efforts—of common dangers, sufferings, and success.

But these considerations, however powerfully they address themselves to your sensibility, are greatly outweighed by those which apply more immediately to your interest. Here every portion of our country finds the most commanding motives for carefully guarding and preserving the union of the whole.

The *north*, in an unrestrained intercourse with the *south*, protected by the equal laws of a common government, finds in the productions of the latter great additional resources of maritime and commercial enterprise, and precious materials of manufacturing industry. The *south*, in the same intercourse, benefiting by the same agency of the *north*, sees its agriculture grow and its commerce expand. Turning partly into its own channels the seamen of the *north*, it finds its particular navigation invigorated—and while it contributes in different ways to nourish and increase the general mass of the national navigation, it looks forward to the protection of a maritime strength, to which itself is unequally adapted. The *east*, in like intercourse with the *west*, already finds, and in the progressive improvement of interior communications by land and water will more and more find, a valuable vent for the commodities which it brings from abroad, or manufactures at home. The *west* derives from the *east* supplies requisite to its growth and comfort; and what is perhaps of still greater consequence, it must of necessity owe the secure enjoyment of indispensable outlets for its own productions, to the weight, influence, and the future maritime strength of the Atlantic side of the Union, directed by an indissoluble community of interest as one nation. Any other tenure by which the *west* can hold this essential advantage, whether derived from its own separate strength, or from an apostate and unnatural connection with any foreign power, must be intrinsically precarious.

While, then, every part of our country thus feels an immediate and particular interest in union, all the parts combined cannot fail to find in the united mass of means and efforts, greater strength, greater resources, proportionably greater security from external danger, a less frequent interruption of their peace by foreign nations; and, what is of inestimable value, they must derive from union an exemption from those broils and wars between themselves, which so frequently afflict neighbouring countries, not tied together by the same government, which their own rivalships alone would be sufficient to produce; but which opposite foreign alliances, attachments, and intrigues, would stimulate and imbitter. Hence, likewise, they will avoid the necessity of those overgrown military establishments, which, under any form of government, are inauspicious to liberty, and which are to be regarded as particularly hostile to republican liberty. In this sense it is, that your union ought to be considered as a main prop of your liberty, and that the love of the one ought to endear to you the preservation of the other.

These considerations speak a persuasive language to every reflecting and virtuous mind, and exhibit the continuance of the union as a primary object of patriotic desire. Is there a doubt whether a common government can embrace so large a sphere? Let experience solve it. To listen to a mere speculation in such a case were criminal. We are authorized to hope that a proper organization of the whole, with the auxiliary agency of governments for the respective subdivisions, will afford a happy issue of the experiment. It is well worth a fair and full experiment. With such powerful and obvious motives to union, affecting all parts of our country, while experience shall not have demonstrated its impracticability, there will always be reason to distrust the patriotism of those who in any quarter may endeavor to weaken its bands.

In contemplating the causes which may disturb our union, it occurs as matter of serious concern that any ground should have been furnished for characterizing parties by geographical discriminations—*Northern* and *Southern*; *Atlantic* and *Western*; whence designing men may endeavor to excite a belief that there is a real difference of local interests and views. One of the expedients of a party to acquire influence within particular districts is to misrepresent the opinions and aims of other districts. You cannot shield yourselves too much against the jealousies and heart-burnings which spring from these misrepresentations; they tend to render alien to each other those who ought to be bound together by fraternal affection. The inhabitants of our western country have lately had a useful lesson on this head. They have seen, in the negotiation by the executive, and in the unanimous ratification by the senate of the treaty with Spain, and in the universal satisfaction of that event throughout the United States, a decisive proof how unfounded were the suspicions propagated among them of a policy in the general government, and in the

Atlantic states, unfriendly to their interests in regard to the Mississippi. They have been witnesses to the formation of two treaties,—that with Great Britain, and that with Spain,—which secure to them everything they could desire, in respect to our foreign relations, towards confirming their prosperity. Will it not be their wisdom to rely for the preservation of these advantages on the union by which they were procured? Will they not henceforth be deaf to those advisers, if such there are, who would sever them from their brethren, and connect them with aliens?

To the efficacy and permanency of your union, a government for the whole is indispensable. No alliances, however strict, between the parts, can be an adequate substitute; they must inevitably experience the infractions and interruptions which alliances at all times have experienced. Sensible of this momentous truth, you have improved upon your first essay, by the adoption of a constitution of government better calculated than your former for an intimate union, and for the efficacious management of your common concerns. This government, the offspring of your own choice, uninfluenced and unawed; adopted upon full investigation and mature deliberation; completely free in its principles; in the distribution of its powers uniting security with energy, and containing within itself provision for its own amendment, has a just claim to your confidence and your support. Respect for its authority, compliance with its laws, acquiescence in its measures, are duties enjoined by the fundamental maxims of true liberty. The basis of our political system is the right of the people to make and to alter their constitutions of government. But the constitution which at any time exists, until changed by an explicit and authentic act of the whole people, is sacredly obligatory upon all. The very idea of the power and the right of the people to establish government, presupposes the duty of every individual to obey the established government.

All obstructions to the execution of the laws, all combinations and associations, under whatever plausible character, with the real design to direct, control, counteract, or awe, the regular deliberations and action of the constituted authorities, are destructive of this fundamental principle, and of fatal tendency. They serve to organize faction; to give it an artificial and extraordinary force; to put in the place of the delegated will of the nation the will of party, often a small, but artful and enterprising minority of the community; and according to the alternate triumphs of different parties, to make the public administration the mirror of the ill-concerted and incongruous projects of faction, rather than the organ of consistent and wholesome plans, digested by common counsels and modified by mutual interests.

However combinations or associations of the above description may now and then answer popular ends, they are likely, in the course of time and things, to become potent engines by which cunning, ambitious, and unprincipled men will be enabled to subvert the power of the people, and to usurp for themselves the reins of government; destroying afterwards the very engines which have lifted them to unjust dominion.

Towards the preservation of your government, and the permanency of your present happy state, it is requisite not only that you steadily discountenance irregular opposition to its acknowledged authority, but also that you resist with care the spirit of innovation upon its principles, however suspicious the pretext. One method of assault may be to effect in the forms of the constitution alterations which will impair the energy of the system, and thus to undermine what cannot be directly overthrown. In all the changes to which you may be invited, remember that time and habit are at least as necessary to fix the true character of governments, as of other human institutions; that experience is the surest standard by which to test the real tendency of the existing constitutions of a country; that facility in changes, upon the credit of mere hypothesis and opinion, exposes to perpetual change, from the endless variety of hypothesis and opinion; and remember especially, that, for the efficient management of your common interests, in a country so extensive as ours, a government of as much vigor as is consistent with the perfect security of liberty, is indispensable. Liberty itself will find in such a government, with powers properly distributed and adjusted, its surest guardian. It is, indeed, little else than a name, where the government is too feeble to withstand the enterprises of faction, to confine each member of society within the limits prescribed by the laws, and to maintain all in the secure and tranquil enjoyment of the rights of person and property.

I have already intimated to you the danger of parties in the state, with particular reference to the founding of them upon geographical discriminations. Let me now take a more comprehensive view, and warn you, in the most solemn manner, against the baneful effects of the spirit of party generally.

This spirit, unfortunately, is inseparable from our nature, having its root in the strongest passions of the human mind. It exists under different shapes in all governments, more or less stifled, controlled, or repressed; but in those of the popular form it is seen in its greatest rankness, and is truly their worst enemy.

The alternate domination of one faction over another, sharpened by the spirit of revenge natural to party dissension, which in different ages and countries has perpetrated the most horrid enormities, is itself a frightful despotism. But this leads at length to a more formal and permanent despotism. The disorders and miseries which result, gradually incline the minds of men to seek security and repose in the absolute power of an individual; and, sooner or later the chief of some prevailing faction, more able or more fortunate than his competitors, turns this disposition to the purpose of his own elevation on the ruins of the public liberty.

Without looking forward to an extremity of this kind, (which, nevertheless, ought not to be entirely out of sight,) the common and continual mischiefs of the spirit of a party are sufficient to make it the interest and duty of a wise people to discourage and restrain it.

It serves always to distract the public councils, and enfeeble the public administration. It agitates the community with ill-founded jealousies and false alarms; kindles the animosity of one part against another; foments occasional riot and insurrection. It opens the door to foreign influence and corruption, which finds a facilitated access to the government itself through the channels of party passion. Thus the policy and will of one country are subjected to the policy and will of another.

There is an opinion that parties in free countries are useful checks upon the administration of the government, and serve to keep alive the spirit of liberty. This, within certain limits, is probably true; and in governments of a monarchical cast, patriotism may look with indulgence, if not with favour, upon the spirit of party. But in those of the popular character in governments purely elective, it is a spirit not to be encouraged. From the natural tendency, it is certain there will always be enough of that spirit for every salutary purpose; and there being constant danger of excess, the effort ought to be, by force of public opinion, to mitigate and assuage it. A fire not to be quenched, it demands a uniform vigilance to prevent its bursting into a flame, lest, instead of warming, it should consume.

It is important, likewise, that the habits of thinking in a free country, should inspire caution, in those intrusted with its administration, to confine themselves within their respective constitutional spheres; avoiding, in the exercise of the powers of one department, to encroach upon another. The spirit of encroachment tends to consolidate the powers of all the departments in one, and thus to create, whatever the form of government, a real despotism. A just estimate of that love of power, and proneness to abuse it, which predominates in the human heart, is sufficient to satisfy us of the truth of this position. The necessity of reciprocal, checks in the exercise of political power, by dividing and distributing it into different depositories, and constituting each the guardian of the public weal against invasions of the other, has been evinced by experiments, ancient and modern; some of them in our country, and under our own eyes. To preserve them must be as necessary as to institute them. If, in the opinion of the people, the distribution or modification of the constitutional powers be, in any particular, wrong, let it be corrected by an amendment in the way which the constitution designates. But let there be no change by usurpation; for though this, in one instance, may be the instrument of good, it is the customary weapon by which free governments are destroyed. The precedent must always greatly overbalance, in permanent evil, any partial or transient benefit which the use can at any time yield.

Of all the dispositions and habits which lead to political prosperity, religion and morality are indispensable supports. In vain would that man claim the tribute of patriotism who should labor to subvert these great pillars of human happiness—these firmest props of the duties of men and citizens. The mere politician, equally with the pious man, ought to respect and to cherish them. A volume could not trace all their connection with private and public felicity. Let it simply be asked, where is the security for property, for reputation, for life, if the sense of religious obligation desert the oaths, which are the instruments of investigation in courts of justice? And let us with caution indulge the supposition that morality can be maintained without religion. Whatever may be conceded to the influence of refined education on minds of peculiar structure, reason and experience both forbid us to expect that national morality can prevail in exclusion of religious principles.

It is substantially true that virtue or morality is a necessary spring of popular government. The rule, indeed, extends, with more or less force, to every species of free government. Who that is a sincere friend to it can look with indifference upon attempts to shake the foundation of the fabric?

Promote, then, as an object of primary importance, institutions for the general diffusion of knowledge. In proportion as the structure of a government gives force to public opinion, it is essential that public opinion should be enlightened.

As a very important source of strength and security, cherish public credit. One method of preserving it is to use it as sparingly as possible, avoiding occasions of expense by cultivating peace, but remembering, also, that timely disbursements to prepare for danger frequently prevent much greater disbursements to repel it; avoiding, likewise, the accumulation of debt, not only by shunning occasions of expense, but by vigorous exertions in time of peace to discharge the debts which unavoidable wars have occasioned, not ungenerously throwing upon posterity the burdens which we ourselves ought to bear. The execution of these maxims belongs to your representatives; but it is necessary that public opinion should coöperate. To facilitate to them the performance of their duty, it is essential that you should practically bear in mind, that towards the payment of debts there must be revenue; that to have revenue there must be taxes; that no taxes can be devised which are not more or less inconvenient and unpleasant; that the intrinsic embarrassment, inseparable from the selection of the proper objects, (which is always a choice of difficulties,) ought to be a decisive motive for a candid construction of the conduct of the government in making it, and for a spirit of acquiescence in the measures for obtaining revenue which the public exigencies may at any time dictate.

Observe good faith and justice towards all nations; cultivate peace and harmony with all; religion and morality enjoin this conduct; and can it be that good policy does not equally enjoin it? It will be worthy of a free, enlightened, and, at no distant period, a great nation, to give to mankind the magnanimous and too novel example of a people always guided by an exalted justice and benevolence. Who can doubt but that, in the course of time and things, the fruits of such a plan would richly repay any temporary advantages which might be lost by a steady adherence to it? Can it be that Providence has connected the permanent felicity of a nation with its virtue? The experiment, at least, is recommended by every sentiment which ennobles human nature. Alas! it is rendered impossible by its vices!

In the execution of such a plan, nothing is more essential than that permanent, inveterate antipathies against peculiar nations, and passionate attachment for others, should be excluded; and that, in the place of them, just and amicable feelings towards all should be cultivated. The nation which indulges towards another an habitual hatred, or an habitual fondness, is in some degree, a slave. It is a slave to its animosity or to its affection, either of which is sufficient to lead it astray from its duty and its interest. Antipathy in one nation against another disposes each more readily to offer insult and injury, to lay hold of slight causes of umbrage, and to be haughty and intractable when accidental or trifling occasions of dispute occur.

Hence frequent collisions, obstinate, envenomed, and bloody contests. The nation, prompted by ill-will and resentment, sometimes impels to war the government, contrary to the best calculations of policy. The government sometimes participates in the national propensity, and adopts, through passion, what reason would reject; at other times, it makes the animosity of the nation subservient to the projects of hostility, instigated by pride, ambition, and other sinister and pernicious motives. The peace often, sometimes perhaps the liberty, of nations has been the victim.

So, likewise, a passionate attachment of one nation for another produces a variety of evils. Sympathy for the favourite nation, facilitating the illusion of an imaginary common interest in cases where no real common interest exists, and infusing into one the enmities of the other, betrays the former into a participation in the quarrels and the wars of the latter, without adequate inducements or justification. It leads, also, to concessions to the favourite nation of privileges denied to others, which are apt doubly to injure the nation making the concessions, by unnecessarily parting with what ought to have been retained, and by exciting jealousy, ill-will, and a disposition to retaliate, in the parties from whom equal privileges are withheld; and it gives to ambitious, corrupt, or deluded citizens, (who devote themselves to the favourite nation,) facility to betray or sacrifice the interests of their own country without odium, sometimes even with popularity; gilding with the appearances of a virtuous sense of obligation to a commendable deference for public opinion, or a laudable zeal for public good, the base or foolish compliances of ambition, corruption, or infatuation.

As avenues to foreign influence, in innumerable ways, such attachments are particularly alarming to the truly enlightened and independent patriot. How many opportunities do they afford to tamper with domestic factions, to practise the art of seduction, to mislead public opinion, to influence or awe the public councils! Such an attachment of a small or weak towards a great and powerful nation, dooms the former to be the satellite of the latter. Against the insidious wiles of foreign influence, (I conjure you to believe me, fellow-citizens,) the jealousy of a free people ought to be constantly awake, since history and experience prove that foreign influence is one of the most baneful foes of republican government. But that jealousy, too, to be useful, must be impartial, else it becomes the instrument of the very influence to be avoided, instead of a defence against it. Excessive partiality for one foreign nation, and excessive dislike for another, cause those whom they actuate to see danger only on one side, and serve to veil and even second the arts of influence on the other. Real patriots, who may resist the intrigues of the favorite, are liable to become suspected and odious; while its tools and dupes usurp the applause and confidence of the people to surrender their interests.

The great rule of conduct for us, in regard to foreign nations, is, in extending our commercial relations, to have with them as little political connection as possible. So far as we have already formed engagements, let them be fulfilled with perfect good faith. Here let us stop.

Europe has a set of primary interests, which to us have none, or a very remote relation. Hence, she must be engaged in frequent controversies, the causes of which are essentially foreign to our concerns. Hence, therefore, it must be unwise in us to implicate ourselves, by artificial ties, in the ordinary vicissitudes of her politics, or the ordinary combinations and collisions of her friendships or enmities.

Our detached and distant situation invites and enables us to pursue a different course. If we remain one people, under an efficient government, the period is not far off when we may defy material injury from external annoyance; when we may take such an attitude as will cause the neutrality we may at any time resolve upon to be scrupulously respected; when belligerent nations, under the impossibility of making acquisitions upon us, will not lightly hazard the giving us provocation; when we may choose peace or war, as our interest, guided by justice, shall counsel.

Why forego the advantages of so peculiar a

situation? Why quit our own to stand upon foreign ground? Why, by interweaving our destiny with that of any part of Europe, entangle our peace and prosperity in the toils of European ambition, rivalship, interest, humor, or caprice?

It is our true policy to steer clear of permanent alliances with any portion of the foreign world; so far, I mean, as we are now at liberty to do it; for let me not be understood as capable of patronizing infidelity to existing engagements. I hold the maxim no less applicable to public than to private affairs, that honesty is always the best policy. I repeat, therefore, let those engagements be observed in their genuine sense. But, in my opinion, it is unnecessary, and would be unwise, to extend them.

Taking care always to keep ourselves, by suitable establishments, on a respectable defensive posture, we may safely trust to temporary alliances for extraordinary emergencies.

Harmony, and a liberal intercourse with all nations, are recommended by policy, humanity, and interest. But even our commercial policy should hold an equal and impartial hand; neither seeking nor granting exclusive favors or preferences; consulting the natural course of things; diffusing and diversifying by gentle means the stream of commerce, but forcing nothing; establishing with powers so disposed, in order to give trade a stable course, to define the rights of our merchants, and to enable the government to support them, conventional rules of intercourse, the best that present circumstances and natural opinion will permit, but temporary, and liable to be, from time to time, abandoned or varied, as experience and circumstances shall dictate; constantly keeping in view that it is folly in one nation to look for disinterested favors from another; that it must pay with a portion of its independence for whatever it may accept under that character; that by such acceptance it may place itself in the condition of having given equivalents for nominal favors, and yet of being reproached with ingratitude for not giving more. There can be no greater error than to expect or calculate upon real favors from nation to nation. It is an illusion which experience must cure, which a just pride ought to discard.

In offering to you, my countrymen, these counsels of an old, affectionate friend, I dare not hope they will make the strong and lasting impression I could wish—that they will control the usual current of the passions, or prevent our nation from running the course which has hitherto marked the destiny of nations. But if I may even flatter myself that they may be productive of some partial benefit, some occasional good; that they may now and then recur to moderate the fury of party spirit; to warn against the mischiefs of foreign intrigue; to guard against the impostures of pretended patriotism; this hope will be a full recompense for the solicitude for your welfare by which they have been dictated.

How far, in the discharge of my official duties, I have been guided by the principles which have been delineated, the public records and other evidences of my conduct must witness to you and to the world. To myself, the assurance of my own conscience is, that I have at least believed myself to be guided by them.

In relation to the still subsisting war in Europe, my proclamation of the 22d of April, 1793, is the index to my plan. Sanctioned by your approving voice, and by that of your representatives in both houses of Congress, the spirit of that measure has continually governed me, uninfluenced by any attempt to deter or divert me from it.

After deliberate examination, with the aids of the best lights I could obtain, I was well satisfied that our country, under all the circumstances of the case, had a right to take, and was bound in duty and interest to take, a neutral position. Having taken it, I determined, as far as should depend upon me, to maintain it with moderation, perseverance, and firmness.

The considerations which respect the right to hold this conduct, it is not necessary on this occasion to detail. I will only observe, that, according to my understanding of the matter, that right, so far from being denied by any of the belligerent powers, has been virtually admitted by all.

The duty of holding a neutral conduct may be inferred, without anything more, from the obligation which justice and humanity impose on every nation, in cases in which it is free to act, to maintain inviolate the relations of peace and amity towards other nations.

The inducements of interest for observing that conduct will be best referred to your own reflections and experience. With me, a predominant motive has been to endeavor to gain time to our country to settle and mature its yet recent institutions, and to progress without interruption to that degree of strength and constancy which is necessary to give it, humanly speaking, the command of its own fortune.

Though, in reviewing the incidents of my administration, I am unconscious of intentional error, I am nevertheless, too sensible of my defects not to think it probable that I may have committed many errors. Whatever they may be, I fervently beseech the Almighty to avert or mitigate the evils to which they may tend. I shall also carry with me the hope that my country will never cease to view them with indulgence; and that, after forty-five years of my life dedicated to its service, with an upright zeal, the faults of incompetent abilities will be consigned to oblivion, as myself must soon be to the mansions of rest.

Relying on its kindness in this as in other things, and actuated by that fervent love towards it, which is so natural to a man who views in it the native soil of himself and his progenitors for several generations,—I anticipate, with pleasing expectation, that retreat in which I promise myself to realize, without alloy, the sweet enjoyment of partaking, in the midst of my fellow-citizens, the benign influence of good laws under a free government— the ever favorite object of my heart, and the happy reward, as I trust, of our mutual cares, labors, and dangers.

www.ingramcontent.com/pod-product-compliance
Lightning Source LLC
Chambersburg PA
CBHW020302240426
43673CB00039B/681